# Telecourse Study Guide to The Business File

# Telecourse Study Guide to The Business File

## Raymond F. Attner
Brookhaven College

for the
## Dallas County Community College District

Accompanying text:
## Introduction to Business, Third Edition
by Straub and Attner

## PWS-KENT Publishing Company
Boston

**PWS–KENT**
Publishing Company

Editor: **Read Wickham**
Assistant Editor: **Diane Miliotes**
Production Editor: **Leslie Baker**
Interior Design: **Karen Keohan**
Cover Designer: **Hannus Design Associates**
Manufacturing Manager: **Linda Siegrist**

## Dallas County Community College District
## Center for Telecommunications

Director, Educational Resources: **Pamela K. Quinn**
Director, Production Services: **Bob Crook**
Director, Instructional Services: **Ted Pohrte**
Director, Information and Distribution: **Jeff Moyers**
Director, Business Services: **Dorothy Clark**

*The Business File* telecourse is produced by the Dallas County Community College District in association with Florida State Department of Education, Northern Illinois Learning Resources Cooperative, The Pennsylvania State University, and Southern California Consortium, and in cooperation with PWS-KENT Publishing Company.

PWS-KENT Publishing Company is a division of Wadsworth, Inc.

Printed in the United States of America

1 2 3 4 5 6 7 8 9 — 92 91 90 89 88

# Preface

Welcome to the world of business—its excitement, its multiple environments, its challenges. What is business? Is it the private enterprise system? Is it producing and marketing a product or service? Is it managing the resources of the organization? Is it functioning in an environment influenced by government regulation, organized labor, and an unpredictable, and often volatile, economy? The answer to all these questions is "Yes." These are all elements of a business and the world of business. But how do they relate? What is business *really* all about?

*The Business File* has been designed to provide answers to these questions. The twenty-eight lessons of *The Business File* will enmesh you in the inner workings of a business: its functions, the critical concepts and processes involved in business, the challenges facing business, and the influences that can affect business decision making.

The approach in designing the course has been to build logically your business experience. Initially you are exposed to the climate of business: the private enterprise system, from both a business and an economic perspective, and an examination of the businesses that make up business. The content then becomes more focused, shifting to the examination of a business: its legal forms and the processes involved in organizing and managing a business. The course quickly gains momentum as you explore the functions or tasks that are common to all businesses: the management of production, marketing, finance, risk, information, and accounting. Once you know the inner workings of a business, decisions that must be made, and activities that have to be accomplished, you are prepared to examine the external environments that affect business and within which business must function: labor, government regulation, social responsibility, law, and the economy. Finally, you will learn about the challenges facing business: high technology, productivity, and business on an international scale.

The objective of *The Business File* is to provide you with the opportunity to see the business environment and the workings of a business as an insider. You should understand what happens within the functions of a business. You should know what activities take place, what processes are critical, and why. You should *feel* the pulse of business. I hope *The Business File* will result in a better understanding of business and the world of business.

# The Learning System

The learning system you will use as you work through *The Business File* has three components: a telecourse study guide, a text, and television programs. Together they provide an integrated learning system. Let's examine each of the components for its purpose and application to your learning experience.

# Telecourse Study Guide

The telecourse study guide is intended to be your road map through *The Business File*. It serves as the starting point for each lesson's learning experience, telling you when and how to use the text and television segment. It will serve as your point of reference for reading assignments, key terms, viewing experience, and individual testing. Each lesson within the telecourse study guide includes the following elements.

- **Learning Objectives.** The Learning Objectives are what you are expected to know when you complete the lesson. They serve as the basis for examination. They are the main points emphasized in the Overview section of the study guide, in the reading assignment, and in the television program.
- **Overview.** The Overview provides a narrative summary of the lesson. Its purpose is to focus your attention on the critical elements developed in the lesson by integrating material from the text reading assignment with information from the television portion of the lesson. In some instances, the Overview includes material to provide a bridge between textbook material and the television program.
- **Reading Assignment.** The Reading Assignment, given under the heading Before Viewing in each lesson, provides the theoretical information needed to master the Learning Objectives from each lesson.
- **Key Terms.** The Key Terms are words or phrases you should be able to define to use appropriately in the business environment.
- **Television Focus Questions.** The Television Focus Questions provide a guide to the major points discussed by the program host, businesspeople, and academicians. The name of the guest is mentioned in the focus question to help you identify the person and the point he or she is making. Before viewing, use these questions to focus your attention on the important concepts included in the television program. After viewing, use these questions as a review. If you have questions about the material presented, view the program a second time.
- **Self-Test.** The Self-Test should give you an indication of how well you have mastered the Learning Objectives of each lesson. The tests are composed of seven true/false and seven multiple choice questions. Each question is designed to test your knowledge of the material discussed in the text, the telecourse study guide, or the television program.

- **Business in Action and Your Business Portfolio.** These exercises give you an opportunity to investigate or to apply the concepts and principles presented in each lesson. The Business in Action exercises will help you investigate how the concepts and processes introduced in each lesson are applied in the business environment. Through a series of investigative assignments, you will have the opportunity to observe business in action. Your Business Portfolio is designed to have you apply the concepts and processes presented in the lesson. By participating in the experiences, reflecting on them, and analyzing the results, you will have the opportunity to become involved in business. These exercises can be used as individual case assignments or as the basis for group discussions. Your instructor will provide directions for the application of the Business in Action and Your Business Portfolio exercises.
- **Answer Key.** The Answer Key located at the end of each lesson serves as the feedback device for the Self-Test. The answer for each question is referenced to a section of the text (T), the telecourse study guide (TG), or the television program itself (V).

# Text

The text for this course is *Introduction to Business,* Third Edition, by Joseph T. Straub and Raymond F. Attner. The purpose of the text is to provide a theoretical knowledge base for your introduction to business. Included in the text are vocabulary definitions, explanations of concepts, practical illustrations of business in action, and profiles of businesspeople.

# Television Programs

The television programs give you access to the world of business. In each television program, the major concepts and processes included in the lesson are explained initially by college professors. Then, leading businesspeople discuss the practical application of the concepts and processes. In addition, the camera gives you the opportunity to travel to the environments where the action takes place, facilitates your learning by presenting difficult concepts in graphic form, and presents real-life documentary case problems.

Using television for learning is not like watching a comedy series or a sporting event. At first you will have to concentrate on *active* watching. It is very easy to slip into the passive, half-viewing state used when watching television solely for entertainment.

To maximize your learning from the television programs, you may need to watch the programs more than once. In most instances you will have a chance to review the lesson in an alternate time period or watch video cassettes of the lesson at the learning center or other facility on campus.

If you have an audio recorder available, tape the audio portion of the program as you are viewing it. After you have watched the program and can visualize it, the audio portion is an excellent source for review. If you have any questions about content or wish additional information, contact your faculty advisor at the campus where you are enrolled. He or she is a resource for you to use.

## How to Use the Telecourse Study Guide: Suggested Study Sequence

This learning system has been carefully developed to utilize the best features of each of the three components. To progress comfortably, please follow this study sequence in the telecourse study guide.

- **Review the Lesson Objectives.** The Lesson Objectives will tell you what you are supposed to learn during each lesson. The test questions will evaluate your mastery of these objectives.

- **Read the Overview.** The Overview will assist you in concentrating on the major topics to be developed in the lesson. In some instances supplementary material has been included to provide a bridge between textbook material and television discussions.

- **Read the Text Assignment.** The reading assignment for each lesson provides you with the theoretical concepts on which the television program is based.

- **Define the Key Terms.** Write out workable definitions for your Key Terms.

- **Review the Television Focus Questions.** The Television Focus Questions will help you become comfortable with the sequence of topics introduced in the television program. Look over the Television Focus Questions before viewing, take notes on the questions while viewing, and after watching the program go over the answers to complete the questions.

- **Complete the Self-Test.** The Self-Test will provide feedback on your understanding of the lesson material. Questions have been developed from the text, telecourse study guide, and television program. Check your answers by using the Answer Key at the end of each lesson. If you did not answer the questions correctly, review the referenced material. All answers in the Answer Key are referenced to the text, the telecourse study guide, or the television program.

- **Complete the Business in Action and Your Business Portfolio Exercises.** Your Business Portfolio exercises are intended for your personal use. Complete these exercises as you progress through the course and use them as a basis for completing your own learning process. The Business in Action exercises can also be completed as part of your personal learning experiences or they can be assigned by your instructor for evaluation and discussion. Both exercises are valuable tools for increasing your understanding of the lesson material.

## Acknowledgments

Whenever media are used, many individuals who have made enormous contributions, both tangible and intangible, do not receive credit. The latter category is sometimes the most important because it usually consists of the emotional support needed to carry forth the tangible results. The following people have contributed in one or both of the categories.

— Jim Lee Morgan, Pat Cancro, Marty Yopp, and Jack Kapoor, the National Advisory Committee who created the "right stuff," provided emotional support, and represented their constituencies well

— Paul Bosner, the producer, who designed the telecourse format and worked the long hours to make it all happen

— Bob Crook, the executive producer, who pulled the right strings to make it all come together, when it had to

— Shirley Spitler, the thread who kept us all straight, made the right connections, and closed the loops

— Greg Bader and Janet Fulton, the eye and the ear of the telecourse series, whose skills allowed us to see business in a unique perspective

— Linda Sparks, who kept the words flowing, and Sandy Adams, who made the words fit

— Gina Nelson, Gene Hilton, Barry West, Bob Meyer, Diane Waggoner, Marilyn Sullivan, Bob Rasp, Diane McNulty, Everett Hall, David Roylance, Ann Keen, Nora Manning, Mike Kissner, Rick Efflandt, and Bruce Hogarth, who kept the fires burning in the M&M Center and provided resources and support

— Donnelle Attner, partner and counselor

*Ray Attner*

# Contents

# Telecourse Study Guide
# to The Business File

# Lesson

1

# The Business of Business

## Learning Objectives

After studying this lesson, you should be able to:

1.  Describe the different types and sizes of firms that compose the American business system.
2.  Describe the role of goods-producing and services-producing firms in the American business system.
3.  Explain the concept of the private enterprise system.
4.  Describe the role of profit and competition in the private enterprise system.
5.  Relate the concept of the private enterprise system to capitalism.
6.  Relate the concept of supply and demand to the private enterprise system.
7.  Explain the evolution of the American business system.

## Overview

Business and businesses are everywhere, and everyone is a part of the business scene. Do you have an image in your mind of what "business" is? Is it corporations like Xerox, International Business Machines, Procter & Gamble? If it is, you're right, but there is more to business than these large corporations. It is the neighborhood service station, the beauty shop, the pizza place, the grocery store. It also includes the truck lines that haul your goods, the airlines, and yes, the "mom-and-pop" store just around the corner. Businesses do come in all shapes and sizes, but despite the variations in size and activity, each is a business because each is an organization engaged in producing goods and services to make a profit.

When you examine the operations of business further, businesses can be classified as either goods-producing or services-producing firms. Goods-producing firms (manufacturing, mining, and construction firms) play a significant role in the business environment by producing goods—commodities that have a physical presence. Services-producing firms (transportation firms, insurance companies, dry cleaners) provide services—activities that benefit consumers or other businesses.

The environment in which these businesses operate is known as the private enterprise system. The private enterprise system is an economic system where both the resources necessary for production and the businesses are owned by private individuals, not by public institutions like the government. This system is based on four principles or rights:

— The right to private property (individuals have the right to buy, own, use, and sell property as they see fit).
— The right of freedom of choice (individuals have the right to decide what type of work to do, where to work, and how and where money is spent).
— The right to profit (the person who takes the chance in starting the business by investing is guaranteed the right to all profits).
— The right to compete (people have the freedom to compete with others).

Profit and competition are the cornerstones of the private enterprise system. Profit is the difference between a business's total revenues or sales receipts and the total of its production costs, operating expenses, and taxes. It serves as a reward for risk taking, measures success, and provides the guidelines for directing investment into a business. The second cornerstone, competition, affects both the businessperson and the consumer. For the businessperson competition is the key to being and staying sharp in the marketplace. It forces companies to alter pricing and product strategies, have the product where and when it is needed, and place a premium on product improvement. The consumer in turn benefits from this competition by having a better quality and variety of product available.

In economic terms, the private enterprise system is called capitalism—an economic system where the factors of production are in private hands. Initially the private enterprise system was pure capitalism or a market economy, one in which economic decisions were made freely according to the forces of supply and demand.

In pure capitalism the marketplace, or supply and demand, is in operation. Consumers demand more of a product as its price decreases. On the other hand, producers are more willing to supply a product that can be sold for a higher price. The converse is also true. Consumers demand less of a product as its price increases while suppliers are willing to supply less of a product as its price decreases. In pure capitalism the two factors of supply and demand will balance each other out in such a way that some middle ground, called an equilibrium price, will be achieved. Thus the marketplace is regulated by the interaction of buyers and sellers. Each person behaves in the best interests of society, as if guided by an invisible hand.

Over time the private enterprise system has evolved into one of mixed capitalism, which is an economic system based on a market economy with limited government involvement. The American business system did not just happen. It has evolved over a number of years, going through identifiable stages or eras. The four stages or eras include the colonial era, the Industrial Revolution era, the growth of modern industry stage, and the international power stage.

## Before Viewing

— Review the Overview and Learning Objectives for this lesson.
— Read the following assignment from the text *before* watching the television segment:
  Straub and Attner, *Introduction to Business*, Third Edition.
  Chapter 1, pages 2–8, 11, 12, 16–18.
— Define the Key Terms listed in the next section.
— Review the Television Focus Questions and take notes on the questions when viewing the program.

## Key Terms

Terms are referenced to a page of the text.

**business** (p. 5)
**capitalism** (p. 11)
**entrepreneur** (p. 9)
**entrepreneurship** (p. 9)
**goods** (p. 6)
**laissez-faire *or* hands-off approach** (p. 12)

**mixed capitalism** (p. 12)
**private enterprise system** (p. 7)
**profit** (p. 7)
**pure capitalism *or* market economy** (p. 11)
**services** (p. 6)

## Television Focus Questions

1. What five elements does Professor Calvin Kent of Baylor University include in his description of the private enterprise system?
2. What are the four rights or foundations of the private enterprise system according to Professor Calvin Kent?
3. What two essential elements of an entrepreneur are noted by Professor Calvin Kent?
4. What are an entrepreneur's roles in the private enterprise system according to Professor Calvin Kent?
5. What does the private enterprise system mean to Walter Durham, president of MESBIC Financial Corporation?

6. What does Walter Durham state that the private enterprise system does for the consumer?

7. What role does profit play in the private enterprise system according to Walter Durham? What role does profit play with entrepreneurs?

8. What does Walter Durham say is the impact of competition on the consumer?

9. What does the private enterprise system mean to Mo Siegel, president of Celestial Seasonings?

10. What consumer benefits of the private enterprise system are described by Mo Siegel?

11. What does Mo Siegel say is the role of profit?

12. What does profit allow Mo Siegel to do?

13. What example is provided by Mo Siegel to describe the effect of competition on Celestial Seasonings? What has competition forced him to do?

14. How does the law of supply and demand regulate the market according to Professor Calvin Kent? How is equilibrium reached?

15. Why does Professor Calvin Kent describe the determination of equilibrium in the marketplace as the "invisible hand"?

**View the television program "The Business of Business."**

# After Viewing

- Review and answer the Television Focus Questions. If you are uncertain of the information, or missed a point, view or listen to the program again.
- Review the Key Terms from your text and be sure you understand the Learning Objectives for this lesson.
- Take the Self-Test to check your understanding of the concepts presented in this lesson. Compare your answers to the Answer Key located at the end of the lesson. If you answered incorrectly, the key provides a reference point so you can review the material.
- Extend your learning by completing the Business in Action and Your Business Portfolio sections of the lesson.

# Self-Test

## True/False

  T F 1. The American business system is composed of a wide variety of businesses.

  T F 2. A goods-producing firm develops concepts and ideas— nontangible commodities.

T   F   **3.** According to Professor Calvin Kent of Baylor University, the private enterprise system is characterized by decisions made in the marketplace as opposed to state planning.

T   F   **4.** The right of freedom of choice applies to the individual's right to decide what work to do, where to work, and how and where money is spent.

T   F   **5.** According to Professor Calvin Kent, an entrepreneur is a person who has vision and capital.

T   F   **6.** In pure capitalism, as opposed to mixed capitalism, the government plays a dominant role.

T   F   **7.** The colonial era in the evolution of American business is characterized by agricultural production as a basis of commerce.

## Multiple Choice

1. Which of the following is an example of a services-producing firm?
   a. hat manufacturer
   b. computer manufacturer
   c. lumber mill
   d. insurance company

2. According to Walter Durham, president of MESBIC Financial Corporation, what does the private enterprise system mean?
   a. government intervention
   b. opportunity and freedom
   c. profit and taxes
   d. ambition and reward

3. According to Mo Siegel, president of Celestial Seasonings, which of the following describes the role of profit in the private enterprise system?
   a. It is a measuring device.
   b. It implies success.
   c. It drives the system.
   d. It pays for government expenditures.

4. Which of the following is true about competition?
   a. It results in cutthroat tactics.
   b. It may mean rushing the product onto the market.
   c. It is one of the cornerstones of the private enterprise system.
   d. It lessens the quality of products.

5. Which of the following is the economic system referred to as the private enterprise system?
   a. capitalism
   b. communism
   c. neocapitalism
   d. socialism

6. In pure capitalism the marketplace is
   a. dominated by a few large firms.
   b. regulated by the interaction of buyers and sellers.
   c. controlled by goods-producing organizations.
   d. pressured by price instability.
7. Which of the following is a phase or era of American business?
   a. the colonial era
   b. the Industrial Revolution era
   c. the growth of modern industry era
   d. all of the above

## Business in Action

This exercise is designed to have you investigate the rights and values of the private enterprise system.

**Step 1.** Identify a small business and obtain an interview with the *owner.*

**Step 2.** In your interview ask the following questions:

— What does the private enterprise system mean to you?
— What does the private enterprise system allow you to do in your business?
— What are the limitations of the private enterprise system?
— What role does competition play in the conduct of your business?
— What does the private enterprise system do for the consumer?
— What does competition in the private enterprise system do for the consumer?

**Step 3.** Identify a large business and obtain an interview with the owner or upper-level manager. Ask the questions outlined in Step 2.

**Step 4.** Record your answers to both interviews.

**Step 5.** Compare the answers to your interview questions with those given by the two entrepreneurs in the television program "The Business of Business," noting similarities and differences. Summarize the similarities and differences.

## Your Business Portfolio

This exercise is designed to have you participate in the private enterprise system and experience the operations of a market economy.

**Step 1.** Either organize or actively participate in a multiparticipant or multi-family garage sale.

**Step 2.** Before the garage sale participate in a discussion that determines:

— How goods are to be priced.
— Who will initially determine the price of the goods being sold.
— How price adjustments, if needed, will be made during the sale.
— Who will make the price adjustments, if needed, during the sale.
— How profits are to be determined.
— How profits from the sale are to be distributed.

**Step 3.** During the garage sale observe the interactions of the buyers and sellers in the marketplace. Specifically note the following:

— What goods were ideally priced (i.e., sold immediately without the buyer questioning the price)?
— What goods required a price adjustment by the seller?
— Was the decision to change the price made with the first customer or after a number of customers?
— What influenced the decision to change the price?
— Were the goods reduced in price near the end of the sale? Why?

**Step 4.** After the sale note the following:

— What goods remained unsold?
— Were these goods that
    **a.** people showed little demand for or
    **b.** had prices that were seen as unrealistic?
— What could have been done to market these goods?

**Step 5.** Record the results of your observations by answering each question in Steps 2, 3, and 4. Discuss your observations about the private enterprise system and the market economy.

## Answer Key

The Answer Key provides a reference for each question: T (text page), TG (Telecourse Guide page), or V (video program).

### True/False

1.  **T** (T 5, TG 1, V)
2.  **F** (T 6, TG 1, 2)
3.  **T** (V)

### Multiple Choice

1.  **d** (T 6, TG 2)
2.  **b** (V)
3.  **c** (V)

4. **T** (T 7, TG 2, V)
5. **F** (V)
6. **F** (T 12, TG 2, V)
7. **T** (T 17)

4. **c** (T 8, TG 2, V)
5. **a** (T 11, TG 2, V)
6. **b** (T 12, V)
7. **d** (T 17, 18, TG 3)

# Lesson

## 2

# Comparative Economic Systems: Is Capitalism the Best?

## Learning Objectives

After studying this lesson, you should be able to:

1. Identify and explain the four factors of production.
2. Describe the role of the four factors of production in an economic system.
3. Describe the capitalistic economic system in terms of the four factors of production.
4. Describe the socialistic economic system in terms of the four factors of production.
5. Describe the communistic economic system in terms of the four factors of production.
6. Explain how the following economic questions are answered in each of the economic systems:
    - What is to be produced?
    - How much is to be produced?
    - Who is to produce it?
    - Who is going to get it?

## Overview

Where do the cars we drive, the clothes we wear, and the radios we listen to come from? Still bigger questions to be answered include (1) How was the decision made that these goods were to be produced? and (2) How many were to be produced? The obvious answer to these questions is businesses—businesses made the goods, and in the process the decisions were made on what goods and how many goods. But, this answer only leads to more questions: Why these goods and not others? Is there a controlling mechanism or system that makes these decisions? The answer to all these questions can be found by examining capitalism from a different perspective. The previous lesson was designed to explore the private enterprise system or capitalism from a business perspective—what makes it function and what are its foundations, challenges, and mechanisms. In this lesson we will examine the private enterprise system or capitalism from an economic perspective—as an economic system in comparison to other economic systems.

The starting point is to look at what makes up the goods and services. The factors of production are the resources used to provide the goods and services for society. There are four factors of production: land (natural resources), labor (total human resources), capital (total of tools, equipment, machinery, and buildings), and entrepreneurship (the group of skills and risk taking required to combine the other factors). These are blended together to produce goods and services.

The goods and services produced by combining the factors of production can vary. The factors can be used to produce cars, blue jeans, records, stereos, or houses in different quantities. The factors also can be used to produce land-moving equipment, office buildings, and printing presses. How these decisions are made is determined by the type of economic system a society functions within.

The economic system serves as the allocator of resources and, ultimately, the determining factor in what goods are produced, how much is produced, who is to produce the goods, and who will receive the goods (how the goods are distributed). There are three major types of economic systems: capitalism, socialism, and communism. Each one (1) allocates the factors of production and (2) provides answers to the basic economic questions (what, how many, who will produce it, and who will receive the goods). Each one has its philosophical goals, costs, and benefits. The economic system that American business flourishes under is known as the private enterprise system, or capitalism. Under capitalism the factors of production are privately owned. All the economic questions are answered by the price mechanism in the marketplace or by supply and demand. There are two types of capitalism: pure capitalism and mixed capitalism. The American economic system is not pure capitalism; it is mixed capitalism in which there is government involvement.

Other countries have chosen to operate under communism or socialism as economic systems. In a communist economic system the allocation of the factors of production are controlled by the government. All economic questions are ultimately determined by the government. Socialism is an economic system that incorporates control of basic industries by the government and much private ownership. Both the factors of production and the economic questions are addressed by a combination of these two controlling elements.

## Before Viewing

— Review the Overview and Learning Objectives for this lesson.
— Read the following assignment from the text *before* watching the television segment:
  Straub and Attner, *Introduction to Business*, Third Edition,
  Chapter 1, pages 8–16.
— Define the Key Terms listed in the next section.
— Review the Television Focus Questions and take notes on the questions when viewing the program.

## Key Terms

Terms are referenced to a page of the text.

**capital** (p. 9)
**capitalism** (p. 11)
**communism** (p. 13)
**economic system** (p. 11)
**entrepreneur** (p. 9)
**entrepreneurship** (p. 9)
**factors of production** (p. 8)
**gross national product (GNP)**
  (p. 14)

**household** (p. 9)
**labor** (p. 8)
**laissez-faire** *or* **hands-off approach**
  (p. 12)
**land** (p. 8)
**mixed capitalism** (p. 12)
**pure capitalism** *or* **market economy**
  (p. 11)
**socialism** (p. 14)

## Television Focus Questions

1. Who controls the means of production in a capitalistic economy according to Professor Lester Thurow of the Massachusetts Institute of Technology?

2. How does Professor Milton Friedman of Stanford University state that the basic economic questions are answered in capitalism? How is capitalism organized?

3. What does Professor Paul Samuelson of MIT mean by saying, "It's a system of voting but it's not a political system"? By what process do people acquire their vote in a capitalist economic system?

4. What two areas of government intervention does Professor Thurow cite that distinguish modified capitalism from pure capitalism?

5. What effect on the market system does Professor Friedman note results from government intervention in modified capitalism?

6. How does the establishment of a minimum wage prevent the market system from working according to Professor Friedman?

7. Who does Professor Samuelson state owns the resources in a communist

**11**

economic system?

8. Under a communist economic system how are the resources allocated according to Professor Samuelson?

9. How does Professor Lester Thurow describe the role of the state in communism?

10. How are the economic questions answered under communism, according to Professor Friedman?

11. What does Professor Friedman mean when he says, "That is how communism works in principle"?

12. How does Professor Samuelson describe socialism?

13. What does Professor Thurow state was the idea behind socialism? What does the government own? How do workers earn and spend money?

14. What industries does Professor Thurow give as examples that are owned by governments in a socialist economy?

15. How does Professor Thurow state a socialist economy allocates resources?

**View the television program "Comparative Economic Systems: Is Capitalism the Best?"**

# After Viewing

— Review and answer the Television Focus Questions. If you are uncertain of the information, or missed a point, view or listen to the program again.

— Review the Key Terms from your text and be sure you understand the Learning Objectives for this lesson.

— Take the Self-Test to check your understanding of the concepts presented in this lesson. Compare your answers to the Answer Key located at the end of the lesson. If you answered incorrectly, the key provides a reference point so you can review the material.

— Extend your learning by completing the Business in Action and Your Business Portfolio sections of the lesson.

# Self-Test

## True/False

T  F  1. Entrepreneurship is the factor of production that includes the total human resources of an organization.

T  F  2. An economic system regulates the economy.

T  F  3. According to Professor Lester Thurow of the Massachusetts Institute of Technology, capitalism is an economic system based on private control of the means of production.

T  F   4. In economic terms a household is any person or group of people living under the same roof and functioning as an economic unit.

T  F   5. Pure capitalism depends on each person behaving in the best interests of society.

T  F   6. Communism is an economic system in which the government controls the factors of production.

T  F   7. Comparing economic systems is difficult because they are organized differently.

## Multiple Choice

1. Which of the following is a factor of production?
   a. utility
   b. labor
   c. energy
   d. transportation

2. An economic system
   a. is controlled by politicians.
   b. efficiently allocates resources.
   c. is a method used to solve problems.
   d. is a method used to allocate resources.

3. According to Professor Paul Samuelson of the Massachusetts Institute of Technology, socialism is
   a. identical to communism.
   b. not an economic system.
   c. a halfway house between capitalism and communism.
   d. requires more study.

4. Which of the following is one of the economic questions?
   a. When will a good be produced?
   b. How many goods will be distributed?
   c. What goods will be produced?
   d. Where will the goods be produced?

5. With mixed capitalism the government has become involved in the economic system
   a. by necessity.
   b. through the channels of distribution.
   c. as a result of public concern.
   d. through government taxation and spending.

6. Which of the following is a yardstick for measuring the performance of an economy?
   a. the amount of consumer goods
   b. the amount of capital goods

      c. its gross national product
      d. consumer satisfaction
  7. Which of the following is true about economic systems?
      a. They all perform equally.
      b. The goals and conditions under which they operate are different.
      c. They have the same goals.
      d. They all have the same areas of emphasis.

# Business in Action

This exercise is designed to have you investigate capitalism as an economic system.

**Step 1.** Identify a manufacturing firm and interview the owner or a top-level manager.

**Step 2.** In your interview ask the following questions:

- What natural resources are required to produce this product? (factor of production: land)
- What labor resources are required to produce this product? (factor of production: labor)
- What capital resources are required to produce this product? (factor of production: capital)
- What entrepreneurial resources are required to produce this product? (factor of production: entrepreneurship)
- Where do you acquire these resources?
- How do you acquire these resources?
- What limits your ability to acquire the needed resources?
- How do you determine what to produce?
- How do you determine how much to produce?
- How do you determine where and to whom to distribute the product?

**Step 3.** Record your answers to each question and analyze the results.

**Step 4.** Discuss your observations regarding:

- Who controls the factors of production.

- What determines if the company can acquire the factors of production.

- How these basic economic questions are answered:
      a. What is produced?
      b. How much is produced?
      c. Who is going to get the product?

# Your Business Portfolio

This exercise is designed to involve you with the factors of production.

**Step 1.** Identify a product that you would like to manufacture in your home for ultimate sale to consumers.

**Step 2.** For this product identify the required factors of production, the sources of those factors, and the means of acquiring the factors. Specifically:

- Factor of Production: Capital
    a. What tools, equipment, and machinery are required?
    b. What financial resources are required?
    c. Where can these resources be acquired?
    d. How can these resources be acquired?

- Factor of Production: Land
    a. What natural resources are required?
    b. What component parts are required?
    c. Where can these resources be acquired?
    d. How can these resources be acquired?

- Factor of Production: Labor
    a. What human resources are required?
    b. Where can these resources be acquired?
    c. How can these resources be acquired?

- Factor of Production: Entrepreneurship
    a. What entrepreneurial skills are needed?
    b. How are these skills used to combine the other three factors of production?
    c. Where can these resources be acquired?
    d. How can these resources be acquired?

**Step 3.** Record your answers to each question and analyze the results.

**Step 4.** Discuss your observations about the factors of production and their allocation under capitalism.

# Answer Key

The Answer Key provides a reference for each question: T (text page), TG (Telecourse Guide page), or V (video program).

True/False

1. **F** (T 9, TG 10, V)
2. **F** (T 11)

Multiple Choice

1. **b** (T 8, 9, TG 10, V)
2. **d** (T 11, TG 10, V)

**15**

3.  **T** (V)
4.  **T** (T 9)
5.  **T** (T 12)
6.  **T** (T 13, TG 10)
7.  **T** (T 14)

3.  **c** (V)
4.  **c** (T 11, 12, TG 10, V)
5.  **d** (T 12)
6.  **c** (T 14)
7.  **b** (T 14)

# Lesson

## 3

# Business Opportunities:
# Large and Small

## Learning Objectives

After studying this lesson, you should be able to:

1. Recognize that the business system is a mixture of large and small businesses.
2. Distinguish between the size of large and small businesses according to sales, assets, number of employees, and geographic effect.
3. Describe the roles of large and small business in the business system.
4. List and describe the advantages and disadvantages of large business.
5. List and describe the advantages and disadvantages of small business.
6. Explain how firms perform the same managerial and operational activities regardless of size.
7. Recognize that the potential exists for a small business to evolve into a large business.

## Overview

The previous lessons have focused on an overview of the business environment, the private enterprise system, and an analysis of how this business environment functions as an economic system. Each was intended to provide an understanding of the environment that businesses function in.

Having seen the overall environment, we need to explore the businesses—big and small—that make up the business scene; the roles they play, the strengths they have in the marketplace, and the observable similarities and differences they have. In other words, we are going to take a look at the fabric of business itself.

You may have an image of "business" that includes organizations like Sears, International Business Machines (IBM), and Mobil Oil. These firms *are* part of what business is, but it is equally important to recognize your neighborhood gas station, record shop, sporting goods dealer, or meat market as part of the business scene. It is not made up of only large businesses or small businesses. The business scene is a blend of businesses of every size. Business is business.

But what makes a business large or small? Part of the answer is found in the type of ownership, impact in its field of operations, scope of geographic operation, amount of sales, and number of employees. Small business usually is independently owned and operated. It is not dominant in its field of operations, and the geographic area of its operations is primarily local. In terms of employees and sales, the size standard varies according to the industry. In a retail and service area, a small business is one with less than $2 million in annual sales while wholesalers are described as small when sales are less than $9 million annually. In the manufacturing field, businesses with less than 250 employees are small.

The point is not one of size, however. Whether a business is large or small, it is a business. Each identifies and fills a special niche; each plays a unique role in the business setting; and each brings observable strengths to the marketplace.

Specifically, small business:

— Dominates in the service industries (repair, cleaning, grocery, contracted services) and the distribution industry (retail stores and wholesalers).
— Performs services not only for the consumer but also for large business in addition to serving as the ultimate link from the large business to the consumer.
— Creates jobs and develops business opportunities. Because it fills niches in the marketplace, small business provides an opportunity for employing people as well as for providing the impetus to create new businesses to solve other businesses' problems.
— Provides the environment to foster entrepreneurship and innovation. Small business can provide this environment because it is unencumbered by complicated decision-making processes or it is better able to focus its energies on a specific area.
— Encourages larger firms to remain competitive in the marketplace. Because small business can adapt, place a premium on creativity and innovation, and develop new products and methods in a minimum amount of time, it keeps larger firms competitive.
— Fosters an environment in which people can receive a well-rounded development opportunity. Because of the lack of specialization within small companies, individuals may experience more diverse business activities than if they worked for a large company. These developmental opportunities include diversified activities as well as the chance to become more intimately involved in the decision-making processes.

**18**

On the other hand, large business:

— Dominates in the manufacturing, transportation, communications, and utilities industries.
— Creates systems and structure to develop ideas and bring them to the ultimate consumer in the quantity desired.
— Serves as an ultimate customer for small businesses and in many instances actually creates the need for small businesses to come into existence.
— Provides the initial training in technology, marketing, and finance for individuals who eventually become the founders of small businesses.
— Provides direct employment for hundreds and thousands of people. In addition, large business indirectly provides employment for millions more by being able to produce goods and services that are bought and sold throughout the economic system.

Once again, the point is that business is business. Both large and small businesses have their niches and play roles in the business scene. Additionally, each brings its strengths to the marketplace for the benefit of the ultimate consumer and business itself.

Small business has strengths and advantages. It has the ability to:

1. Respond to changes in market conditions and needs, and quickly develop production, marketing, and service activities to meet those conditions and needs.
2. Make personal contact and develop relationships with customers and employees that facilitate identifying needs and implementing change.
3. Be independent in operations and have minimal government regulations.

On the other hand, small business often suffers in the marketplace because it:

1. Has a shortage of financial resources.
2. Is not always able to attract and maintain an adequate staff of specialists.
3. Lacks adequate management talent. The management team most often consists of the owner/manager who may lack either the specialized management skills needed by the business or the necessary general business knowledge.

Large business has the following strengths and advantages:

1. A large base of financial resources with which to operate. The initial capital is larger, and large business has an easier time raising additional capital.
2. An ability to attract and retain specialized personnel.

**19**

3. A larger base of management expertise and more managers capable of overseeing the specialized areas of a business.
4. Access to resources for research and development programs.

As with small business, large business has limitations. Specifically it:

1. Often lacks the ability to be responsive and flexible to changes in the marketplace. As a result of its size, big business often develops layers of decision-making steps that slow the decision-making process.
2. Has a tendency to stifle creativity with red tape and numerous systems.
3. Must comply with numerous government regulations. This not only helps to create the layers of red tape but also diverts resources from the company.

Despite their obvious advantages and disadvantages, it is important to note that *both* small and large businesses are present in the marketplace. Each serves needs and creates products and services to satisfy new needs. In doing this each must perform the same functions and activities. Regardless of size, all businesses must create a product or service; market that product or service; account for the financial transactions; hire, train, and evaluate people; and acquire financing. All businesses must perform the same management functions—each must plan what it wants to accomplish, organize its resources, acquire the people to operate the business, guide the people toward the objectives, and monitor progress. The only difference between a large business and a small business is the degree of sophistication involved in its functions and activities. In a small business the owner may do it all, while in a large business there is a staff of specialists to accomplish the tasks.

There is one final point to remember in our examination of the businesses that compose the business scene. Large businesses did not just happen, they evolved from little businesses. Someone once started a small business and, through good management, the business grew. A big business is not big because it is big; it started small and was guided to its present state.

## Before Viewing

— Review the Overview and Learning Objectives for this lesson.
— Read the following assignment from the text *before* watching the television segment:
Straub and Attner, *Introduction to Business*, Third Edition, Chapter 1, pages 4–5.
— Review the Television Focus Questions and take notes on the questions when viewing the program.

Please note: There are no Key Terms for this lesson.

# Television Focus Questions

1. What three characteristics of small business are noted by Professor Justin Longenecker of Baylor University?
2. What specific industries does Professor Longenecker cite as the domain of small businesses? Of large businesses? What two roles do small businesses play?
3. What reason does Jack Baum, owner of Newport's Restaurant, give for choosing to go into business for himself rather than work for someone else?
4. What is the specific disadvantage given by Jack Baum of a small business? What is the specific advantage?
5. What reason does Jack Baum cite for limiting the growth of his business?
6. What two advantages of a large business are described by Michael Jordan, president of Frito-Lay, Inc.? What is a specific disadvantage?
7. What reason does Michael Jordan cite for working in a large business rather than working for himself?
8. What statement is made by Professor Justin Longenecker regarding the differences in the functions of big and small businesses?
9. What activities or functions are required in a small business, according to Jack Baum?
10. What specific role does Jack Baum play in the accomplishment of the functions?
11. What functions does Michael Jordan identify as necessary at Frito-Lay?
12. How are these functions accomplished at Frito-Lay? What is Michael Jordan's role?
13. What differences between large and small businesses exist in the performance of the functions as noted by Professor Longenecker?
14. According to Michael Jordan, how has Frito-Lay evolved?
15. What are Jack Baum's plans for his restaurant? What specific ingredient is needed to accomplish the objectives?

**View the television program "Business Opportunities: Large and Small."**

# After Viewing

– Review and answer the Television Focus Questions. If you are uncertain of the information, or missed a point, view or listen to the program again.
– Be sure you understand the Learning Objectives for this lesson.
– Take the Self-Test to check your understanding of the concepts presented in this lesson. Compare your answers to the Answer Key located at the end

of the lesson. If you answered incorrectly, the key provides a reference point so you can review the material.
— Extend your learning by completing the Business in Action and Your Business Portfolio sections of the lesson.

## Self-Test

### True/False

**T    F    1.** In describing the American business scene it is appropriate to say, "Business as we know it is conducted only by big business."

**T    F    2.** A small business is one that is *not* dominant in its field of operations.

**T    F    3.** According to Professor Justin Longenecker of Baylor University, a major role of small businesses is to provide financing for large businesses.

**T    F    4.** One strength large business brings to the marketplace is its ability to acquire a large base of capital.

**T    F    5.** A specific role of large business is to provide direct employment for hundreds of thousands of individuals.

**T    F    6.** According to Jack Baum, owner of Newport's Restaurant, a specialized group of managers is responsible for performing all the functions and activities of his company.

**T    F    7.** With their ability to acquire capital resources, large businesses begin operations as large businesses.

### Multiple Choice

**1.** Which of the following describes the American business scene or environment?
   **a.** Small businesses dominate.
   **b.** Large businesses dominate.
   **c.** Business is a blend of small and large businesses.
   **d.** Small and large businesses are equally represented.

**2.** Which of the following describes the specific niche of small business? Small business
   **a.** dominates the transportation industry.
   **b.** dominates the distribution industry.
   **c.** plays a significant role in manufacturing.
   **d.** plays a major role in the communications industry.

3. According to Professor Justin Longenecker of Baylor University, a small business
   a. is dominant in its field.
   b. has multiple ownership.
   c. conserves its resources.
   d. is local in operations.
4. One of the strengths of small business in the marketplace is the ability to
   a. minimize research time.
   b. maximize the use of resources.
   c. negotiate contracts.
   d. be flexible to changes in market conditions.
5. The specific advantage of a small business, according to Jack Baum of Newport's Restaurant, is the
   a. quality of employees attracted.
   b. ability to see most of what is going on in the business.
   c. flexibility in geographic location.
   d. patronage of friends.
6. Regardless of the size of the business, all businesses
   a. utilize people identically.
   b. perform the same functions or activities.
   c. have the same degree of sophistication in performing activities.
   d. must maintain inventories at a proper level.
7. According to Michael Jordan, president of Frito-Lay, Inc., the functions of the business are
   a. his major tasks.
   b. diversified throughout the country.
   c. completed by first-line managers.
   d. performed by specialists.

## Business in Action

This exercise is designed to have you investigate the nature of the functions and activities performed by large and small businesses.

**Step 1.** Identify two businesses in the same industry, one large and one small (a small retailer, manufacturer, or car dealer and a large retailer, manufacturer, or car dealer).

**Step 2.** Interview a top-level manager or owner of each business and ask the following questions:

– What functions (i.e., accounting, personnel, marketing) are necessary in your business?

— Who performs these functions for your business?
— If you don't perform the functions, what is your role in relationship to the performance of those functions?
— How many employees do you have, and how are they assigned according to these functions?

**Step 3.** Summarize your findings by answering each question in Step 2 and discuss the statement, "Business is business. The same functions need to be performed regardless of size."

# Your Business Portfolio

This exercise is designed to involve you in the demands of evolving a small business into a large business.

**Step 1.** Identify a hobby or special interest you have that you could convert into a business opportunity.

**Step 2.** List the activities that need to be performed in the business.
Example: Accounting for finances
         Producing the product
         Selling the product
         Purchasing materials
         Developing contracts

**Step 3.** For the activities identified, explain who would perform each.
Example: Accounting for finances
         Contracted bookkeeping service

**Step 4.** Your business (photography, car repair, handicrafts, secretarial service, carpentry) has been well received by potential customers. In fact, it is more than you can continue to do under your present arrangement. (It has quadrupled in size.) You can no longer perform your assigned functions.

— Identify what physical facilities would be required to operate your business in.
— Identify who would perform the functions initially assigned to you.
— Identify how many people would be necessary to operate a business four times larger than the present one.
— Identify what additional functions would be necessary to have when you started to hire employees.
— Identify what demands would be placed on you as an owner/manager rather than an owner/doer.

— Identify which special functions or activities would now need to be performed by contracted services.

**Step 5.** Summarize your findings by writing an explanation for each area identified in Step 4.

# Answer Key

The Answer Key provides a reference for each question: T (text page), TG (Telecourse Guide page), or V (video program).

<table>
<tr><td colspan="2">True/False</td><td colspan="2">Multiple Choice</td></tr>
<tr><td>1.</td><td>F (TG 18, V)</td><td>1.</td><td>c (TG 18, V)</td></tr>
<tr><td>2.</td><td>T (TG 18)</td><td>2.</td><td>b (TG 18, V)</td></tr>
<tr><td>3.</td><td>F (V)</td><td>3.</td><td>d (V)</td></tr>
<tr><td>4.</td><td>T (TG 19)</td><td>4.</td><td>d (TG 19)</td></tr>
<tr><td>5.</td><td>T (TG 19)</td><td>5.</td><td>b (V)</td></tr>
<tr><td>6.</td><td>F (V)</td><td>6.</td><td>b (TG 20, V)</td></tr>
<tr><td>7.</td><td>F (TG 20)</td><td>7.</td><td>d (V)</td></tr>
</table>

# Lesson

## 4

# Forming a Business: Proprietorships and Partnerships

## Learning Objectives

After studying this lesson, you should be able to:

1. Explain the nature of a sole proprietorship as a form of business ownership.
2. Describe the process involved in creating a sole proprietorship.
3. Describe the advantages and disadvantages of a sole proprietorship as a form of business ownership.
4. Explain the nature of a partnership as a form of business.
5. Describe the process involved in creating a partnership.
6. Explain the purposes and elements of a partnership agreement.
7. Describe the advantages and disadvantages of a partnership.
8. Identify and distinguish between the two major types of partnerships.
9. Explain the purposes and characteristics of a joint venture.
10. Distinguish between silent, secret, nominal, and dormant partners.

## Overview

All businesses, regardless of whether they are large or small, goods-producing or services-producing, have to make a decision on which legal form of ownership they will utilize. There are three basic options to choose from—sole proprietorship, partnership, or corporation. Which one is best? There is no single answer to that question. It will depend on the type and scope of operations, the nature of the product or service, and the particular goals of the business. Each is a viable alternative. This lesson will focus on sole proprietorships and partnerships.

The sole proprietorship is a business owned by one individual. In the eyes of the law, the owner and the company in a sole proprietorship are inseparable. It requires no formal authorization to begin business operations. A business-person can decide on a business venture, check on local ordinances, obtain a sales tax number, and begin operations.

In addition to its ease of formation, a sole proprietorship has other advantages, including retaining all the profits from the business, freedom in decision making, personal satisfaction from personal achievement, the ability to easily dissolve the business if desired, and tax advantages of having the business income taxed as personal income.

Despite having numerous advantages, a sole proprietorship has some obvious disadvantages, including unlimited liability, limited funds for expansion of the business, limited business and management skills, difficulty in attracting employees, and a limited life.

A second form of business ownership is a partnership. A partnership is an association of two or more people who are co-owners of a business for profit. Although a partnership may be entered into by simply discussing a business proposition with a prospective partner or partners and reaching an agreement, it is recommended that partnerships be formalized with an articles of partnership agreement. In essence, this is a contractual agreement that establishes the legal relationship between partners.

Partnerships, as with proprietorships, have advantages and disadvantages. On the plus side, a partnership is easy to form, pools the knowledge and skills of the partners, makes more funds available, provides the ability to attract and retain employees, and has profit taxed as personal income of the partners. On the negative side, partnerships have unlimited liability for the partners, face the potential of conflict between partners, and are difficult to dissolve.

There are two major types of partnerships. One type, known as a general partnership, is an association of two or more people, each with unlimited liability, who are actively involved in the business. The second type of partnership is a limited partnership. It is a partnership arrangement in which the liability of one or more of the partners is limited to the amount of the assets they have invested in the firm.

Although general and limited partnerships are the two major types of partnership arrangements, a third type exists that is designed for short-term projects—a joint venture. It is a partnership established by two or more persons to carry out a specific adventure or undertaking. It is usually dissolved after the objective has been achieved.

In addition to partners being identified by the types of partnerships, partners often are referred to by other names: silent, secret, dormant, or nominal. A silent partner is a partner who is not active in the management of the firm. A secret partner is a partner who may be an active manager but does not want his or her identity revealed to the general public. A dormant or sleeping partner is a partner who is both secret and silent and is only interested in investing funds in the company for financial profit. A nominal partner is an individual who is neither a part-owner of the partnership nor an active participant in the firm's affairs.

## Before Viewing

— Review the Overview and Learning Objectives for this lesson.
— Read the following assignment from the text *before* watching the television segment:
Straub and Attner, *Introduction to Business*, Third Edition, Chapter 2, pages 28–47.
— Define the Key Terms listed in the next section.
— Review the Television Focus Questions and take notes on the questions when viewing each program.

## Key Terms

Terms are referenced to a page of the text.

**articles of partnership** (p. 36)           **nominal partner** (p. 45)
**dormant *or* sleeping partner** (p. 45)   **partnership** (p. 36)
**general partner** (p. 40)                       **secret partner** (p. 44)
**general partnership** (p. 39)                 **silent partner** (p. 44)
**joint venture** (p. 42)                          **sole proprietorship** (p. 31)
**limited partner** (p. 41)                        **unlimited liability** (p. 34)
**limited partnership** (p. 40)

## Television Focus Questions

1. How does Professor Calvin Kent of Baylor University describe a sole proprietorship?
2. What reason is given by Professor Calvin Kent for a businessperson to consider a sole proprietorship as a form of business?
3. What does Professor Kent mean by "Hang out your shingle, and you're in business"?
4. What reasons are cited by David McCoy, owner of McCoy's Photography, for selecting a sole proprietorship as a form of business?
5. What specific advantage of a sole proprietorship is noted by David McCoy?
6. What disadvantages of a sole proprietorship are mentioned by David McCoy?
7. Would David McCoy select a sole proprietorship form again? Why?
8. How does Professor Calvin Kent define a partnership? What amount of responsibility and authority does each partner have?
9. What is the major advantage of a partnership according to Professor Kent? What is the major disadvantage?
10. What reasons are given by Sue Hanna and Roberta Christie, partners in the Craft Studio, for forming a partnership?

11. What is the major advantage of the partnership noted by both Roberta Christie and Sue Hanna?

12. What does Sue Hanna think could lead to problems in a partnership?

13. What three factors does Sue Hanna state that it takes to make a partnership work?

14. What is Professor Calvin Kent describing when he states, "They are really two or more people functioning as one. That is the general partnership"? What role does a limited partner play in a limited partnership?

15. What process does Professor Kent recommend for forming a partnership?

16. According to Professor Kent, what circumstances would favor the selection of each of the business forms of ownership?

**View the television program "Forming a Business: Proprietorships and Partnerships."**

# After Viewing

— Review and answer the Television Focus Questions. If you are uncertain of the information, or missed a point, view or listen to the program again.

— Review the Key Terms from your text and be sure you understand the Learning Objectives for this lesson.

— Take the Self-Test to check your understanding of the concepts presented in this lesson. Compare your answers to the Answer Key located at the end of the lesson. If you answered incorrectly, the key provides a reference point so you can review the material.

— Extend your learning by completing the Business in Action and Your Business Portfolio sections of the lesson.

# Self-Test

## True/False

T  F  1. In a sole proprietorship, the business and the proprietor have separate liability.

T  F  2. According to David McCoy of McCoy Photography, a sole proprietorship's major advantage is the freedom in decision making.

T  F  3. The process of creating a sole proprietorship requires approval by the city council.

T  F  4. A partnership is an association between two or more people who are co-owners of a business for profit.

T   F   5. A partnership is required by law to create an articles of partnership agreement.

T   F   6. In a limited partnership all the partners have limited liability.

T   F   7. A nominal partner is neither a part owner of the partnership nor an active participant in a firm's affairs.

## Multiple Choice

1. Which of the following is an advantage of a sole proprietorship form of business?
   a. ability to attract employees
   b. perpetual life
   c. ease of dissolution
   d. The sole proprietor is taxed separately from the company.

2. Which of the following is an advantage of a partnership?
   a. pools knowledge and skills
   b. provides for better equipment
   c. allows for a larger geographic area of business
   d. attracts publicity

3. Which of the following is *not* an item to be included in an articles of partnership agreement?
   a. type of stock issued
   b. distribution of profits
   c. responsibilities of the partners
   d. date of partnership

4. According to Professor Calvin Kent, which of the following is the major disadvantage of the partnership form of business?
   a. difficulty in dissolving the business
   b. unlimited liability
   c. the risk involved
   d. limited life

5. Which of the following is an obligation of a general partner under the Uniform Partnership Act?
   a. to distribute all profits equally
   b. to distribute all losses equally
   c. to provide personal financial statements
   d. to work for the partnership for a share of the profits rather than pay

6. Which of the following does *not* describe a joint venture?
   a. It is utilized in international business.
   b. It is common in real estate.
   c. It is designed for long-range projects.
   d. It is designed for a specific undertaking.

7. A partner who assumes no active role in managing the firm, but who may be known to the general public as a partner, is a
   a. silent partner.
   b. secret partner.
   c. calculated partner.
   d. nominal partner.

# Business in Action

This exercise is designed to have you investigate a general partnership.

**Step 1.** Individually interview each partner of a general partnership. In your interview ask the following questions:

- Why did each partner agree to form a partnership?
- What did each partner bring to the partnership in terms of skills and financial resources?
- What areas of responsibility does each partner have in the operation?
- Does an articles of partnership exist for this business?
- From each partner's perspective, what is the major advantage of a partnership?
- From each partner's perspective, what is the major disadvantage of a partnership?

**Step 2.** Record the responses.

**Step 3.** Compare the information received from each partner for consistency. Discuss your findings.

**Step 4.** Compare your interview information with the lesson information in the text and the television program. Discuss your findings.

# Your Business Portfolio

This exercise is designed to have you evaluate the advantages and disadvantages of a sole proprietorship, a general partnership, and a limited partnership as a business ownership form.

**Step 1.** Identify a hobby you have that you could turn into a business operation. Consider gardening, macramé, woodworking, typing, auto repair, personal computer skills, and other possibilities.

**Step 2.** Evaluate a sole proprietorship, a general partnership, or a limited partnership as a form of legal ownership for your business venture.

— For a Sole Proprietorship
  a. Evaluate your technical skills.
  b. Evaluate your business skills (i.e., accounting, marketing, organizational ability).
  c. Evaluate the financial resources necessary to operate the business as well as your ability to provide these.
  d. Analyze your answers.

— For a General Partnership
  a. Evaluate what skills you would seek in a partner—technical or business or both.
  b. Evaluate what responsibility areas should be assigned to each partner.
  c. Evaluate the financial resources you need and would expect from a partner.
  d. Evaluate what expectations you would have of a partner in terms of honesty, time commitment, and cooperation.
  e. Evaluate your own skills to work with another person as a partner.
  f. Analyze your answers.

— For a Limited Partnership
  a. Evaluate what financial resources are needed for the organization.
  b. Evaluate what profit percentage you are willing to share with a limited partner.
  c. Analyze your answers.

**Step 3.** Summarize your responses in the three areas.

**Step 4.** Determine which form is the most appropriate and explain your answer.

## Answer Key

The Answer Key provides a reference for each question: T (text page), TG (Telecourse Guide page), or V (video program).

### True/False

1. **F** (T 34)
2. **T** (V)
3. **F** (T 33, TG 27, V)
4. **T** (T 36, TG 27)
5. **F** (T 36, TG 27, V)
6. **F** (T 41, V)
7. **T** (T 45, TG 27)

### Multiple Choice

1. **c** (T 34, TG 27)
2. **a** (T 36, TG 27)
3. **a** (T 37, 38)
4. **c** (V)
5. **d** (T 40)
6. **c** (T 42, 43, TG 27)
7. **a** (T 44)

# Forming a Business: Corporations

## Learning Objectives

After studying this lesson, you should be able to:

1. Explain the nature of a corporation as a form of business ownership.
2. Describe the process for incorporating a business.
3. Identify and explain the categories of corporations based on place of chartering.
4. Describe the advantages and disadvantages of the corporate form of business.
5. Explain the S corporation form of business.
6. Distinguish between open and close corporations, public and private corporations, and profit and nonprofit corporations.
7. Describe the internal organization of a corporation.
8. Describe the potential combination of corporations: acquisition, merger, and amalgamation.

## Overview

There are three forms of legal ownership: sole proprietorship, partnership, and a corporation form of ownership. This lesson will focus on the corporation. A corporation is a legal form of business organization created by a government and considered an entity separate and apart from its owners. It is an artificial person that has been created by law. A corporation can sue or be sued, make contracts, own property, and even be a partner in a corporation.

Unlike a sole proprietorship or partnership, a corporation begins business operations only after a legal process has been completed. The permission to begin operations, in the form of a corporate charter, is granted by the appropriate state official, usually the secretary of state. To receive approval, the incorporators must file an application known as a certificate (articles) of incorporation and meet the state's requirement for the number of persons necessary to form a corporation.

Corporations fit into three categories depending on where they are chartered. A corporation operating in the state in which it is chartered is known as a domestic corporation. In the other states where it operates it is referred to as a foreign corporation. If the corporation chooses to operate in other countries it would be considered an alien corporation.

The corporate form of business has its advantages and disadvantages. The plus side includes limited liability for the stockholders or owners, ease of expansion, ease of transferring ownership, long life or perpetual life depending on the charter, and the ability to hire specialized management. The negatives include the expense and complication involved in organizing the corporation, the multiple taxation faced by corporations, extensive government restrictions and reporting requirements, and lack of personal identification and commitment to corporate goals by employees.

A special form of incorporation is the S corporation. It provides a way of avoiding the tax disadvantage of corporations while enjoying the advantages of incorporating. If the business qualifies as an S corporation it may be taxed as a sole proprietorship, if owned by one stockholder, or as a partnership, if owned by several stockholders. If the owners choose the S corporation, the corporation pays no federal income tax. Instead, the shareholders declare their share of the firm's taxable income as personal income and it is taxed at their personal income rate.

Are all corporations the same? No, a number of elements can be used to distinguish between corporations. Corporations may be classified as open or close. An open corporation is one whose stock can be purchased by anyone who can afford it. A close corporation, on the other hand, is one whose stock cannot be purchased by the general public; it is usually owned by a few individuals. Corporations may also be classified as private or public. A private corporation is organized by individuals, while a public or government corporation is organized by a city, county, state, or federal government to serve a specific segment of the population. Additionally, corporations may be classified as profit or nonprofit corporations. Profit corporations exist to make a profit, while nonprofit ones do not. Instead they are formed to further the interests and objectives of educational, religious, social, charitable, and cultural groups.

A major difference between a sole proprietorship or partnership and a corporation is in the corporation's internal organization. In both the sole proprietorship and partnership the owner and manager are usually the same person or persons. In a corporation ownership and management are separate. The owners of a corporation are the stockholders, but they do not run the business. The authority is given by the stockholders to the board of directors, which they have elected to represent them. The board of directors in turn selects the company officers: president, secretary, and treasurer.

Corporations potentially can be combined with other businesses to achieve profitability, efficiency, and competitiveness. The potential combinations include acquisitions, mergers, and amalgamations. An acquisition results when one corporation buys a controlling interest in another, but both retain their identities. A merger occurs when two or more companies become a single enterprise; the controlling corporation retains its identity and absorbs the other. An amalgamation occurs when one firm combines with others to form an entirely new company; former identities are relinquished.

## Before Viewing

— Review the Overview and Learning Objectives for this lesson.
— Read the following assignment from the text *before* watching the television segment:
  Straub and Attner, *Introduction to Business*, Third Edition, Chapter 3, pages 50–75.
— Define the Key Terms listed in the next section.
— Review the Television Focus Questions and take notes on the questions when viewing each program.

## Key Terms

Terms are referenced to a page of the text.

acquisition  (p. 65)
alien corporation  (p. 56)
amalgamation *or* consolidation
  (p. 69)
bylaws  (p. 57)
certificate (articles) of
  incorporation  (p. 54)
close corporation  (p. 57)
conglomerate merger  (p. 67)
cooperative  (p. 73)
corporate charter  (p. 54)
corporation  (p. 54)
domestic corporation  (p. 56)
foreign corporation  (p. 56)

government *or* public corporation
  (p. 70)
horizontal merger  (p. 66)
limited liability  (p. 60)
merger  (p. 65)
nonprofit corporations  (p. 71)
open corporation  (p. 56)
proxy  (p. 59)
S corporation  (p. 62)
shareholders *or* stockholders
  (p. 54)
stock certificates  (p. 54)
vertical meger  (p. 66)

## Television Focus Questions

1. How does Professor Calvin Kent of Baylor University describe a corporation? What rights does the corporation have?
2. What three reasons are given by Professor Calvin Kent for a business to incorporate?

3. What two times does Professor Kent cite as appropriate to incorporate?

4. What is the major disadvantage of the corporate form according to Professor Kent? What three areas are included as examples?

5. What does Professor Kent note are the demands the corporate form of business makes on the people who run the corporation?

6. What statement is made by Professor Kent regarding the state where a corporation is chartered?

7. Why did Jack Baum, president of Newport's Restaurant, choose to incorporate?

8. What reason is given by Comer Cottrell, president of Pro-Line Corporation, for incorporating?

9. What decisions did Jack Baum have to make in the process of incorporating?

10. Why did Comer Cottrell choose to incorporate in Texas?

11. What practical limitation of the corporate form of business is noted by Jack Baum?

12. What comment is made by Comer Cottrell regarding the value of limited liability as the corporation grows?

13. Has the corporate form of business proved flexible to Jack Baum?

14. What has the flexibility of the corporate form of business allowed Comer Cottrell to accomplish?

15. What does the term perpetual life mean in business terms according to Professor Calvin Kent? What two reasons are given for its importance?

16. What reason is given by Professor Kent for the owners of a corporation being entitled to limited liability?

**View the television program "Forming a Business: Corporations."**

## After Viewing

— Review and answer the Television Focus Questions. If you are uncertain of the information, or missed a point, view or listen to the program again.

— Review the Key Terms from your text and be sure you understand the Learning Objectives for this lesson.

— Take the Self-Test to check your understanding of the concepts presented in this lesson. Compare your answers to the Answer Key located at the end of the lesson. If you answered incorrectly, the key provides a reference point so you can review the material.

— Extend your learning by completing the Business in Action and Your Business Portfolio sections of the lesson.

# Self-Test

## True/False

T   F   **1.** A corporation is an artificial person created by law.

T   F   **2.** If a business wishes to incorporate it can begin business immediately.

T   F   **3.** An advantage of a corporation is its ease of formation.

T   F   **4.** According to Jack Baum, president of Newport's Restaurant, a purpose for incorporating the business was to lessen personal liability.

T   F   **5.** A foreign corporation is one that is chartered in a foreign country.

T   F   **6.** A corporation organized by a city, county, state, or federal government is known as a public corporation.

T   F   **7.** A business combination in which two or more companies become a single enterprise and only the controlling corporation retains its identity is known as an acquisition.

## Multiple Choice

**1.** Which of the following is an element of the incorporation process?
   **a.** bank loans
   **b.** stock loans
   **c.** certificate (articles) of incorporation
   **d.** hiring management

**2.** Which of the following is an advantage of the corporate form of business?
   **a.** ability to withstand pressure from creditors
   **b.** attractiveness to investors
   **c.** lack of vulnerability to government control
   **d.** ability to expand through raising capital

**3.** Which of the following describes an S corporation?
   **a.** It is a legal partnership.
   **b.** It is a legal sole proprietorship.
   **c.** It allows the owner or owners to be taxed as a sole proprietorship or partnership.
   **d.** Any company is eligible to be an S corporation.

**4.** A corporation in which the stock can be purchased by anyone who can afford it is
   **a.** a low-priced corporation.
   **b.** a public corporation.
   **c.** an open corporation.
   **d.** a traded corporation.

5. Which of the following describes the internal organization of a corporation?
   a. Management and ownership are identical.
   b. Management is developed from insiders.
   c. Management votes by proxy.
   d. Management and ownership are separate.

6. According to Professor Calvin Kent of Baylor University, the major disadvantage of a corporation is
   a. its inability to change.
   b. it is extremely difficult to set up.
   c. its lack of control.
   d. it requires a major capital investment.

7. A business combination used by corporations that want a reliable supply of parts and materials or a guaranteed market for their products is
   a. an acquisition
   b. a horizontal merger.
   c. an amalgamation.
   d. a conglomerate.

# Business in Action

This exercise is designed to have you investigate the strengths and weaknesses of the corporate form of business.

**Step 1.** Identify a small corporation in your community.

**Step 2.** Interview the owner of that corporation (i.e., the major stockholder). In your interview ask the following questions:

— Why did you choose to incorporate rather than create a sole proprietorship or partnership?
— What is the *major advantage* of the corporate form?
— What is the *major disadvantage* of the corporate form?
— What have been the specific reactions of suppliers, banks, and other creditors to entering into contracts with the corporation?

In addition to these questions determine:

— What the purpose of the corporation is as stated in the corporate charter.
— What the life of the corporation is according to the corporate charter.
— If the corporation is open or close.
— Where the corporation was chartered.

**Step 3.** Record the responses to the questions. .

**Step 4.** Analyze the responses, noting any difference between your interview and the material in the lesson.

## Your Business Portfolio

This exercise is designed to involve you in the process of creating a corporation.

**Step 1.** Identify a hobby or activity that you could consider as a business opportunity.

**Step 2.** Using either the library or a lawyer, research the process for incorporating a business in your state.

**Step 3.** Answer the following questions in writing.

— What paperwork must be completed?
— What specific information is requested in the articles of incorporation?
— How many persons are necessary to incorporate?
— What financial information is necessary?
— What fees are required initially and then annually?
— What reporting requirements are called for by the state?
— Who approves the corporate charter?
— How long does the process take?

**Step 4.** Summarize your responses.

## Answer Key

The Answer Key provides a reference for each question: T (text page), TG (Telecourse Guide page), or V (video program).

True/False

1. **T** (T 54, TG 33, V)
2. **F** (T 54, TG 33)
3. **F** (T 61, TG 34, V)
4. **T** (V)
5. **F** (T 56, TG 34)
6. **T** (T 70, TG 34)
7. **F** (T 65, TG 35)

Multiple Choice

1. **c** (T 54, TG 34)
2. **d** (T 60, TG 34)
3. **c** (T 62, TG 34)
4. **c** (T 56, 57, TG 34)
5. **d** (T 57, TG 34)
6. **b** (V)
7. **a** (T 65)

# Lesson

# Managing Business Organizations

## Learning Objectives

After studying this lesson, you should be able to:

1. Explain why managers are necessary in organizations.
2. Explain the concept of management.
3. Identify and explain the five management functions.
4. Identify and explain the three levels of management in a firm.
5. Explain the universality of management as it relates to the levels of management.
6. Describe the roles managers are required to perform.
7. Describe the three skills—technical, human, and conceptual—required of a manager.
8. Explain the nature of and steps involved in managerial decision making.

## Overview

Regardless of whether a business is legally organized as a sole proprietorship, a partnership, or a corporation, it must be managed. Management as a field of study is seen as "getting things done through people." This means that managing must involve people. People become important as an introduction to the concept of organization. An organization is a group of two or more people that exists and operates to achieve clearly stated, commonly held objectives. The objectives of the organization relate to providing goods and services to its members or others outside the organization. To meet these objectives, it is necessary for the members of an organization to work together—to become a cohesive unit. Without a manager, an organization could not coordinate its members to meet objectives. Each member of the staff could be going in a different direction, believing all along that the job he or she is doing is helping to meet the organization's objectives.

To ensure the success of an organization, a manager is needed. A manager can be the owner, operator, or founder (or all three) of an organization; or it may be someone hired by an organization to give the organization direction—to make decisions and commit its resources (personnel, capital, equipment) to achieve the organizations's objectives. The manager is often a connecting link, a catalyst and a driving force for change, a coordinator and controller in an organization. Management is necessary to every organization.

What do managers do? Management is defined as the process of setting and achieving goals through the execution of the five management functions that utilize human, financial, and material resources. The principle task of a manager is to make decisions, communicate those decisions to others, and to coordinate the efforts of the organization in implementing those decisions. This leads to and is precipitated by the performance of the five managerial functions: planning, organizing, staffing, directing, and controlling.

To a manager:

- *Planning* is looking at the future and determining where your organization wants to be in that future time frame.
- *Organizing* is deciding what work is necessary to achieve the plan, dividing the work into jobs, and arranging it into a structure that establishes operating relationships.
- *Staffing* is attracting good people to an organization and holding onto them.
- *Directing* is providing leadership and building an organizational climate that supports the motivational needs of employees.
- *Controlling* is establishing standards, measuring actual performance to see if the standards have been met, and taking corrective action if required.

Knowing that management involves the performance of the five functions leads logically to the next question—Who are the managers? Regardless of a manager's title (section chief, vice-president, regional manager), managers are divided into three basic categories: top management, middle management, and first-line management.

Top management is responsible for the overall management of the organization. It establishes organizational or companywide objectives or goals and operating policies, and it directs the company's relationships with its external environments. Middle management includes all managers below the rank of vice-president but above supervisory level. They are responsible for implementing top management policies. First-line management is the lowest level of management in the management hierarchy. Their subordinates are nonmanagement workers.

A critical point to remember is that regardless of title, position, or management level, all managers execute the five management functions and work through and with others to achieve their goals. This concept, known as the universality of management, emphasizes that all managers perform the managerial functions; however, the amount of time spent and the degree of emphasis on each function varies according to management level.

To carry out these functions a manager must assume roles. A role is one of several behaviors a manager displays as he or she functions in an organization. In other words, a manager must "wear different hats" as he or she interacts with various members of the organization. Some of the roles required of a manager include figurehead, leadership, liaison, monitor, disseminator, spokesperson, entrepreneur, disturbance handler, resource allocator, and negotiator.

As a manager performs the specific role demands and plans, organizes, staffs, directs, and controls, he or she must draw on three basic skills. These skills, needed by all managers, are technical skill, the knowledge of and ability to use the processes, practices, techniques, or tools of a specific area of responsibility; human skill, the ability to interact with other people successfully; and conceptual skill, the mental ability to view the organization as a whole and to see how the parts of the organization relate to and depend on one another.

Along with managerial roles, skills, and functions, a final element of the management environment is decision making. Decision making, the process of making rational choices among alternatives, is part of all managers' jobs. It is not a separate managerial function, but rather it is a common thread within the five management functions. Managers make decisions constantly as they perform the functions of planning, organizing, staffing, directing, and controlling. To make their decisions, managers utilize a seven-step process. A manager must:

1. Define the problem.
2. Identify the limiting or critical factors.
3. Develop potential alternatives.
4. Analyze the alternatives.
5. Select the best alternative.
6. Implement the solution.
7. Establish a control and evaluation system.

## Before Viewing

— Review the Overview and Learning Objectives for this lesson.
— Read the following assignment from the text *before* watching the television segment:
Straub and Attner, *Introduction to Business,* Third Edition, Chapter 4, pages 80–103.

— Define the Key Terms listed in the next section.

— Review the Television Focus Questions and take notes on the questions when viewing the program.

## Key Terms

Terms are referenced to a page of the text.

**conceptual skill**  (p. 97)            **organization**  (p. 82)
**controlling**  (p. 91)                 **organizing**  (p. 88)
**decision making**  (p. 98)             **planning**  (p. 86)
**directing**  (p. 90)                   **policy**  (p. 87)
**first-line management**  (p. 86)       **procedure**  (p. 88)
**human skill**  (p. 97)                 **role**  (p. 94)
**management**  (p. 84)                  **staffing**  (p. 89)
**management functions**  (p. 84)        **technical skill**  (p. 96)
**management hierarchy**  (p. 85)        **top management**  (p. 85)
**middle management**  (p. 85)           **universality of management**  (p. 92)
**objectives**  (p. 87)

## Television Focus Questions

1. According to Professor George Labovitz of Boston University, why is management important and what is management? What example is provided to illustrate how management works?

2. What point is noted by Professor Labovitz about the significance of management titles?

3. What does Professor Labovitz say that managers are paid to do?

4. Do all managers perform the same functions, according to Professor Labovitz? What difference in the performance of the functions is noted?

5. What does Professor Labovitz mean when he states, "With the broader issue of roles of management there is something more to it than just functions"?

6. What roles does Don Lawhorne, president of Captronics, note that he is required to perform as part of the management job?

7. What three skills do managers need, according to Professor Labovitz?

8. What examples does Lawhorne provide to illustrate each of the three basic managerial skills?

9. What point is made by Professor Labovitz regarding the importance of decision making in a manager's job?

10. What are the two dimensions Lawhorne discusses as keys to good decision making?

11. What example does Tony LaRussa, manager of the Chicago White Sox, provide to illustrate the planning function of management?

12. According to Tony LaRussa, what is the most important role he plays as a manager?

13. What examples are provided by LaRussa to illustrate how he uses each of the three managerial skills?

**View the television program "Managing Business Organizations."**

## After Viewing

— Review and answer the Television Focus Questions. If you are uncertain of the information, or missed a point, view or listen to the program again.

— Review the Key Terms from your text and be sure you understand the Learning Objectives for this lesson.

— Take the Self-Test to check your understanding of the concepts presented in this lesson. Compare your answers to the Answer Key located at the end of the lesson. If you answered incorrectly, the key provides a reference point so you can review the material.

— Extend your learning by completing the Business in Action and Your Business Portfolio sections of the lesson.

## Self-Test

### True/False

T  F  1. A manager can be the owner, operator, or founder of an organization as well as someone hired by an organization to give it a direction.

T  F  2. According to Professor George Labovitz, management is getting things done through people.

T  F  3. First-line management is responsible for supervising both management and nonmanagement employees.

T  F  4. Planning is a continuous function that must be performed as long as the organization exists.

T  F  5. A role is any one of several behaviors a manager displays as he or she functions in the organization.

T  F  6. When Don Lawhorne, president of Captronics, describes working with salespeople he is applying technical skills.

T  F  7. Decision making is the sixth managerial function in addition to planning, organizing, staffing, directing, and controlling.

## Multiple Choice

1. Which of the following describes why a manager is needed? A manager
   a. provides capital.
   b. acts as catalyst.
   c. creates product ideas.
   d. reviews production facilities.

2. Which of the following best describes management?
   a. It is a process of setting and achieving goals.
   b. It is performed by all persons in the organization.
   c. It requires a minimum of resources.
   d. It requires a person to have financial ability.

3. Which of the following is the level of management responsible for overall management in the organization?
   a. regional administrator
   b. first-line management
   c. middle management
   d. top management

4. Which of the following is *not* one of the management functions?
   a. planning
   b. organizing
   c. coordinating
   d. controlling

5. Which of the following describes a middle manager's responsibility for planning?
   a. developing the major purpose of the organization
   b. determining global objectives
   c. translating broad goals into specific goals
   d. scheduling employees

6. Which of the following is one of the three basic managerial skills?
   a. communication skill
   b. negotiation skill
   c. conceptual skill
   d. coordination skill

7. Which of the following is *not* one of the steps in decision making?
   a. Set goals.
   b. Identify limiting factors.
   c. Analyze the alternatives.
   d. Implement the solution.

## Business in Action

This exercise is intended to provide you with an opportunity to investigate the functions, roles, and skills required of all managers.

**Step 1.** Interview a manager of a large corporation. In this interview determine:

- The type of planning the manager is responsible for.
- The subgroups the manager has created to carry out tasks.
- What voice the manager has in interviewing, selecting, orienting, training, and appraising employees.
- How the manager views leadership and motivation.
- What type of control devices he or she has created to monitor the progress of work.
- What roles the manager is required to perform and with whom.
- What skills are necessary from the manager's perspective to successfully manage.

**Step 2.** Record the responses.

**Step 3.** Interview a manager of a small company. (Example: a McDonald's franchise.) In the interview cover the same points you did in Step 1.

**Step 4.** Record the responses.

**Step 5.** Compare the results of each interview.

- What are the similarities?
- What are the differences?
- Is management universal?

## Your Business Portfolio

This exercise is designed to illustrate the importance of management in your life.

**Step 1.** Examine your family interactions to determine the extent of your management job within the family.

- For the Functions of Management
  a. What plans did you create? Examples include budgets, trips, social events, grocery lists.

    **b.** What work units did you organize? An example might be assigning the children to wash windows or to complete yard work—all with separate tasks.

    **c.** What training or appraising was necessary to aid the employees in completing the tasks?

    **d.** What guidance, encouragement, or problem solving did you provide to complete these tasks or any others?

    **e.** What control devices did you establish to make sure your plans had been completed? Examples may include inspecting the work of subordinates and monitoring expenditures in the budget.

— For the Roles of Management

    **a.** What roles were you required to perform to complete your management functions?

    **b.** For whom were these roles performed?

    **c.** Which role was required most frequently?

— For Management Skills

    **a.** What technical skills were utilized in the organizing and directing functions of your management experience?

    **b.** What human skills did you display in completing your management functions and fulfilling your management roles?

    **c.** What conceptual skills did you utilize in planning your work?

**Step 2.** Record your responses to these questions.

**Step 3.** Analyze the responses. Summarize your findings in each category and for your total management experience.

## Answer Key

The Answer Key provides a reference for each question: T (text page), TG (Telecourse Guide page), or V (video program).

### True/False

1. **T** (T 83, TG 41)
2. **T** (V)
3. **F** (T 86, TG 41)
4. **T** (T 87)
5. **T** (T 94, TG 42)
6. **T** (V)
7. **F** (T 98, TG 42)

### Multiple Choice

1. **b** (T 84, TG 41)
2. **a** (T 84, TG 41)
3. **d** (T 85, TG 41)
4. **c** (T 86–91, TG 41, V)
5. **c** (T 94)
6. **c** (T 96, 97, TG 42, V)
7. **a** (T 98–102, TG 42)

# Lesson

## 7

# Creating an Organization

## Learning Objectives

After studying this lesson, you should be able to:

1. Explain the purpose of a formal organization structure.
2. List and describe the steps in the organizing process.
3. Describe the four major forms of departmentalization.
4. Define authority and explain the differences between line, staff, and functional authority.
5. Relate the concept of delegation to authority, responsibility, and accountability.
6. Explain the organizational concepts of span of control, centralization and decentralization, and unity of command.
7. Differentiate among line, line-and-staff, functional, and matrix organization structures.
8. Explain the nature of the informal organization.

## Overview

*Everybody is always telling me what to do. I just wish my orders didn't come from so many directions.*

*They reorganized again! I thought that shipping reported directly to the production manager.*

*I just don't know what is going on. I have been waiting for a decision on promoting Johnson for three months. I just keep getting the runaround. Who's in charge here anyway?*

Do any of these situations seem familiar? If so, you have witnessed unsuccessful attempts to provide a well-defined organizational structure. A company that has taken the time, energy, and money to develop quality plans needs to organize its employees to attain these goals. It must provide a structure for all jobs that makes clear who has responsibility for all tasks and who reports to whom. An organization without structure can result in confusion, frustration, loss of efficiency, and limited effectiveness.

A business is an organization. It is created by owners and managers to achieve a specific goal: to provide a product or service at a profit. In the process of creating the organization, managers develop a framework, a formal organization structure to (1) operate effectively, (2) reach the organization's objectives, and (3) provide a profit. This framework or formal organization structure, establishes the operating relationships of people: who supervises whom, who reports to whom, what departments are formed, and what kind of work is performed in each department.

The previous lesson introduced the functions performed by managers and the necessity of those functions. One of those functions is organizing—the creation and modification of a work structure for a business. The purpose of this lesson is to discuss the elements involved in creating an organization.

The organizing process takes place in all organizations regardless of their size, degree of complexity, or number of employees. In a one-person company, all the activities necessary to achieve the objectives of the company (growth, profit, survival) are identified and accomplished by one person. The company is organized and has a structure. As the company grows, another person is hired. Certain activities are identified and assigned to that person. When this occurs the organization structure changes. There is now a boss-subordinate relationship. Two people are working in different activities.

In a large company, one with hundreds of employees doing different activities, there are many departments. Numerous boss-subordinate relationships exist, and many activities are performed. The bottom line is that organizing is necessary. It provides the framework within which people can function and work can be done.

The formal organization is created by managers who use an organizing process. The organizing process has five steps. Managers must: (1) consider the objectives and plans of the organization; (2) determine the work necessary to accomplish the organizational objectives; (3) classify and group the activities into related areas; (4) assign the work to individuals and delegate appropriate authority; and (5) design a hierarchy of relationships. The result of this process is a complete organization structure. It is shown on an organization chart.

As an organization is created (step 3 in the organizing process) management determines the basic type of departmental design for the organization. This process of creating the basic format or departmental structure is known as departmentalization. Management can choose a departmental design from function, geographic or territorial, product, or customer options.

To successfully guide the organization to its objectives, managers need to understand and apply organizational concepts. Specifically, managers need to understand and use the concepts of authority, delegation, responsibility, accountability, span of control, and centralization and decentralization.

Authority is a manager's tool; it can be described as the right to commit resources (that is to make decisions that commit the organization's resources) or the legal right to give orders (to tell someone to do or not to do something). All managers have authority, but they have different degrees and types of authority based on the level of management and roles they play. There are three different types of authority—line, staff, and functional.

Delegation is a concept describing the downward transfer of formal authority from one person to another. As the company grows and more demands are placed on a manager, or because a manager wishes to develop subordinates, delegation takes place. Managers delegate, or pass, authority to subordinates to facilitate the accomplishment of work using the following sequence of events:

1. Assignment of tasks to the subordinate.
2. Delegation of authority to the subordinate.
3. Acceptance of responsibility by the subordinate.
4. Creation of accountability for the subordinate.

This four-step process should ensure that the process of delegation is clearly understood by the manager and the subordinate. By delegating authority down through the management hierarchy, top managers and successive levels of subordinate managers parcel out decision-making authority and specific tasks to appropriate levels on the organization chart.

Span of control refers to the number of subordinates a manager directly supervises. There is no correct number to be assigned to each manager at the top, middle, or bottom of the organization. The exact number for each manager is determined by (1) the complexity and variety of the subordinates' work, (2) the ability of the manager, (3) the ability and training of the subordinates themselves, and (4) the supervisor's willingness to delegate authority.

Centralization and decentralization refer to a philosophy of organization and management that focuses on either the selective concentration (centralization) or the dispersal (decentralization) of authority within an organization structure.

Managers create formal organization structures for companies to help achieve specific objectives. Because the objectives of the companies will differ as a result of resources, stage of organizational development, and philosophies of management, the type of organization structure necessary to meet these objectives will differ. In addition, as companies and their objectives change, it is often necessary to adopt a new format. Management has four options from which to select:

— The line organization structure (the simplest and oldest form of organization).
— The line-and-staff organization structure (blends into the line organization staff personnel that advise and serve the line managers).

— The functional organization structure (an attempt by management to provide expert technical supervision to operating employees by providing separate supervisors for each task).

— The matrix organization structure (temporarily groups together specialists from different departments or divisions to work on special projects).

What we've examined so far is an organization developed by management— the formal organization. But, functioning within the formal organization is something management did not design: the informal organization. The informal organization is a network of personal and social relationships that arises spontaneously as people associate witih one another in the work environment. It is a self-grouping of people that cuts across the formal organization structure. Although it is not shown on the organization chart, managers need to understand and work with and through the informal organization. If approached correctly it can aid in accomplishing the organization's objectives, provide stability, support the manager, and assist in providing information to members of the organization.

## Before Viewing

— Review the Overview and Learning Objectives for this lesson.
— Read the following assignment from the text *before* watching the television segment:
Straub and Attner, *Introduction to Business*, Third Edition, Chapter 5, pages 106–132.
— Define the Key Terms listed in the next section.
— Review the Television Focus Questions and take notes on the questions when viewing the program.

## Key Terms

Terms are referenced to a page of the text.

**accountability** (p. 119)

**authority** (p. 116)

**centralization** (p. 122)

**chain of command** (p. 114)

**customer departmentalization** (p. 113)

**decentralization** (p. 122)

**delegation** (p. 118)

**departmentalization** (p. 112)

**formal organization** (p. 110)

**functional authority** (p. 117)

**functional departmentalization** (p. 112)

**functional organization** (p. 124)

**geographic** *or* **territorial departmentalization** (p. 112)

**informal organization** (p. 126)

**line authority** (p. 116)

**line organization** (p. 122)

**line-and-staff organization** (p. 123)

**matrix organization** (p. 125)
**organization** (p. 109)
**organization chart** (p. 114)
**product departmentalization**
   (p. 113)

**responsibility** (p. 119)
**span of control** (p. 114)
**staff authority** (p. 116)
**unity of command** (p. 125)

## Television Focus Questions

1. According to Professor Rosemary Pledger of the University of Houston–Clear Lake, what are managers attempting to do when they organize a business?
2. What specific information does Professor Pledger note is revealed by an organization chart? What does it *not* show?
3. What specific value of a line organization structure is cited by Professor Pledger?
4. What reason is given by Professor Pledger for a company to use a line-and-staff organization structure?
5. According to Professor Pledger, what problem is created for the worker with a functional organization structure?
6. How is the matrix structure designed according to Professor Pledger?
7. Where does a manager get his or her authority according to Professor Pledger? What does authority provide a manager?
8. What specific difference is noted by Professor Pledger between line authority and staff authority? Where would staff authority be seen in an organization?
9. What specific application of functional authority is noted by Professor Rosemary Pledger?
10. What two organization concepts does Professor Pledger discuss that enable an organization to function smoothly?
11. What does Walt Humann, president of Hunt Oil Company, note is the value of unity of command and span of control?
12. What does a manager delegate according to Professor Pledger? What is *not* delegated?
13. What three reasons for management to delegate are cited by Humann?

**View the television program "Creating an Organization."**

## After Viewing

- Review and answer the Television Focus Questions. If you are uncertain of the information, or missed a point, view or listen to the program again.
- Review the Key Terms from your text and be sure you understand the Learning Objectives for this lesson.

— Take the Self-Test to check your understanding of the concepts presented in this lesson. Compare your answers to the Answer Key located at the end of the lesson. If you answered incorrectly, the key provides a reference point so you can review the material.

— Extend your learning by completing the Business in Action and Your Business Portfolio sections of the lesson.

## Self-Test

### True/False

T  F  **1.** An organization without structure can result in confusion, frustration, loss of efficiency, and limited effectiveness.

T  F  **2.** Accountability is the obligation to carry out one's assigned duties to the best of one's ability.

T  F  **3.** According to Professor Rosemary Pledger of the University of Houston—Clear Lake, when managers organize a business they are trying to organize resources and activities.

T  F  **4.** As a general rule, the more complex the subordinates' jobs, the fewer number of subordinates the manager should have for a span of control.

T  F  **5.** The line organization is based on direct authority.

T  F  **6.** According to Walt Humann, president of Hunt Oil Company, unity of command provides employees a clear understanding of whom they report to.

T  F  **7.** The informal organization, like the formal organization, is a creation of management.

### Multiple Choice

**1.** Which of the following is established by creating an organization structure?
a. the major means of planning
b. the basis for motivation
c. the interrelationships of the various work units
d. the basis for leadership

**2.** Which of the following is *not* one of the steps in the organizing process?
a. Consider objectives and plans.
b. Determine leadership approaches.
c. Determine the necessary work activities.
d. Classify and group activities.

**3.** Which of the following describes authority?
a. It is limited by the manager's ability.

    b. It is vested in a manager because of the position he or she occupies in the organization.

    c. It depends on resources.

    d. It provides absolute control.

4. Delegation is a concept describing the downward transfer of
    a. responsibility.
    b. tasks.
    c. authority.
    d. unity.

5. A philosophy of organization and management that focuses on the selective concentration of authority within an organization structure is known as
    a. construction.
    b. decentralization.
    c. convergence.
    d. centralization.

6. An organization structure that violates the unity of command principle is the
    a. line structure.
    b. line-and-staff structure.
    c. functional structure.
    d. product structure.

7. According to Dr. Rosemary Pledger of the University of Houston–Clear Lake, a manager delegates
    a. responsibility.
    b. authority.
    c. accountability.
    d. control.

# Business in Action

This exercise is designed to provide the opportunity to investigate the elements of organization.

**Step 1.** Interview the manager of a medium or large organization. In conducting your interview determine:

— What type of organization structure the company uses—line, line-and-staff, functional, or matrix.

— Why that particular structure was selected.

— The basis of departmentalization for the manager's department. Why was that form selected?

— What type or types of authority the manager possesses in the organization.
— How wide the manager's span of control is.
— How this span of control was determined.
— If the principle of unity of command is practiced. If not, what factors interfere with its implementation?
— What role the informal organization plays within the formal organization.

**Step 2.** Record the answers to these questions.

**Step 3.** Analyze and compare the interview answers with the material in this lesson.

**Step 4.** Summarize your findings, noting differences and similarities between theory and practice.

## Your Business Portfolio

This exercise is designed to have you apply the organization process in your own life.

**Step 1.** Identify a sports team, church group, social organization, or community group you are or have been associated with.

**Step 2.** Identify the objectives the group attempts to accomplish.

**Step 3.** For that group:

— Consider the plans and objectives of the organization.

— Determine what activities have to be performed for the group to achieve its objectives. List the activities.

— Classify and group the activities.
  **a.** Group financial activities together.
  **b.** Group purchasing activities together.
  **c.** Group communication activities together.
  **d.** Group membership building activities together.

— Assign the activities to a person and delegate the appropriate authority.

— Design a hierarchy of relationships.

**Step 4.** Answer the following questions:

— What basis for departmentalization was utilized?
— What types of authority are present in your organization structure?

**55**

— What is the span of control?
— What type of organization did you develop?

## Answer Key

The Answer Key provides a reference for each question: T (text page), TG (Telecourse Guide page), or V (video program).

True/False

1. **T** (T 108, TG 49)
2. **F** (T 119)
3. **T** (V)
4. **T** (T 120)
5. **T** (T 122, V)
6. **T** (V)
7. **F** (T 126, TG 51)

Multiple Choice

1. **c** (T 116)
2. **b** (T 110–116, TG 49, V)
3. **b** (T 116, V)
4. **c** (T 118, TG 50, V)
5. **d** (T 122, TG 50)
6. **c** (T 125)
7. **b** (V)

# Lesson

## 8

# Human Resources: Acquisition and Development

## Learning Objectives

After studying this lesson, you should be able to:

1. Explain the nature of identifying and acquiring human resources for an organization.
2. List and describe the steps in the human resources process.
3. Explain the impact of equal employment opportunity and affirmative action on human resources management.
4. Describe the process involved in human resources planning.
5. Describe the internal and external sources for human resources recruitment.
6. Outline the selection process and describe each step.
7. Describe the purposes of an employee orientation program.
8. Describe the methods of employee training.
9. Identify and explain the purposes of and types of performance appraisal.
10. List and explain methods of employee compensation and the application of each form.
11. Describe the different types of employee benefits.

## Overview

In the previous lesson we saw the processes management uses to create and modify organizations for a business. When an organization's structure is initially developed, and as it is continually modified, the work activities identified ultimately form the basis for creating or modifying job positions. The challenge for management is to match personnel with the jobs identified and to provide for their long-range growth and welfare.

Without top quality people to work in and to guide it, an organization has little chance for success and, ultimately, little chance for growth. For an organization to survive and prosper it must be able to identify, select, develop, and retain qualified personnel. The people supply the talent, skills, and knowledge to achieve the organization's objectives. This lesson focuses on the activities involved in acquiring and developing human resources.

Human resources management is the staffing function of the organization. It includes the activities of human resources planning, recruitment, selection, orientation, training, performance appraisal, compensation, and safety. Each activity, though unique, is integrated into the overall human resources process. In turn, these distinct activities are critical to the welfare of an individual and, ultimately, to the organization.

Human resources management and its individual activities do not function in a vacuum. The legal environment influences all aspects of the human resources management process. A major influence is legislation that governs equal employment opportunity and affirmative action. Equal Employment Opportunity legislation is designed to provide an employment environment in which job applicants and present employees are free from discrimination in their pursuit of employment opportunities. Affirmative Action goes beyond equal employment opportunity; it requires an employer to make an effort to hire and promote people in a protected minority.

The activities involved in human resources management should be viewed as a series of interrelated steps that managers and specialists perform to acquire and maintain the right people in the right positions. The human resources process includes human resources planning, recruitment, selection, orientation, training, and performance appraisal. (Compensation and safety are not part of the process but are elements of human resources management.)

Human resources planning includes forecasting the demand for and supply of personnel. It has three parts: (1) forecasting the personnel requirements, (2) comparing the requirements with the talents of present employees, and (3) developing specific plans for how many people to recruit from outside the company or who to train from inside the company.

Recruitment attempts to identify and attract candidates to meet the requirements of anticipated or actual job openings. There are two sources of applicants—internal and external.

Selection is the process of deciding which candidate, out of the pool of applicants developed in recruiting, has the abilities, skills, and characteristics that most closely match job demands. These steps include (1) an application blank, (2) preliminary interview, (3) testing, (4) in-depth interviews, (5) reference checks, and (6) a physical examination. If the applicant successfully completes all phases of the selection process a seventh and final step is taken: (7) an offer of employment is made.

Orientation is a series of activities that gives the new employees information to help them adapt to the organization and their new jobs. Its purpose is to turn "them" (new employees) and "us" (the company) into "we." To accomplish this the program should include (1) an overview on the company, (2) information on benefits, (3) completion of appropriate paperwork, (4) a review of the job description, (5) the opportunity to meet co-workers, and (6) time to spend with the immediate supervisor and to become familiar with the new work environment.

Training supplies the skills, knowledge, and attitudes needed by individuals to improve their abilities to perform their jobs. Several training methods can be used including classroom training, on-the-job training (OJT), and vestibule training.

Performance appraisal is a formal measure or rating of an employee's job performance compared with established job standards. It (1) provides feedback on the success of previous training and discloses the need for additional training, (2) aids in developing plans for improvement, (3) identifies growth opportunities, (4) documents present job performance to provide managers with information to make decisions on salary, promotion, transfer, and termination, and (5) provides the opportunity for formal feedback. A company may use a subjective performance appraisal system or an objective performance appraisal system.

A major responsibility area in human resources management is the compensation of employees. Human resources managers are charged with the job of designing a program to attract and retain qualified applicants. Compensation for a job is based on either time put into a job (wages for hours worked or salary for weeks or months worked) or what is produced on the job (piecework). In addition to the base method of compensation, management can choose to provide a bonus, profit sharing, stock options, and a pension plan. Finally, human resources managers build into the work environment fringe benefits—nonfinancial rewards for employees. These may include insurance, vacation, sick pay, holidays, supplemental child care, and tuition reimbursement.

Human resources management also involves providing for the health and safety of the employees in the work environment. A major influence on this activity is the Occupational Safety and Health Act. This federal law requires most employers to create and maintain safe, healthful working conditions.

# Before Viewing

— Review the Overview and Learning Objectives for this lesson.
— Read the following assignment from the text *before* watching the television segment:
Straub and Attner, *Introduction to Business,* Third Edition,
Chapter 6, pages 134–166.

— Define the Key Terms listed in the next section.
— Review the Television Focus Questions and take notes on the questions when viewing the program.

## Key Terms

Terms are referenced to a page of the text.

**Affirmative Action** (p. 140)
**bonus** (p. 161)
**classroom training** (p. 153)
**commission** (p. 161)
**demotion** (p. 156)
**Equal Employment Opportunity** (p. 139)
**Fair Labor Standards Act** (p. 160)
**fringe benefits** (p. 162)
**human resources forecasting** (p. 141)
**human resources inventory** (p. 141)
**human resources management** (p. 137)
**human resources planning** (p. 140)
**job analysis** (p. 142)
**job description** (p. 142)
**job evaluation** (p. 160)
**job specification** (p. 142)
**layoff** (p. 159)
**objective performance appraisal system** (p. 155)

**Occupational Safety and Health Act** (p. 162)
**on-the-job training (OJT)** (p. 153)
**orientation program** (p. 152)
**pay grades** (p. 161)
**pension plan** (p. 162)
**performance appraisal** (p. 154)
**piecework** (p. 161)
**profit sharing** (p. 161)
**promotion** (p. 156)
**recruitment** (p. 142)
**resignation** (p. 159)
**retirement** (p. 159)
**salary** (p. 161)
**selection** (p. 144)
**separation** (p. 159)
**stock option** (p. 161)
**subjective performance appraisal system** (p. 155)
**termination** (p. 159)
**training** (p. 153)
**transfer** (p. 156)
**vestibule training** (p. 153)
**wages** (p. 161)

## Television Focus Questions

1. How does the job application form fit into the area of human resources management according to Mike Kissner, vice president of human resources for the Cullum Companies?

2. What point does Mike Kissner make concerning the value of human resources to a company?

3. What outside forces does Mike Kissner identify that influence hiring and developing people? What reason is given to have a self-imposed affirmative action program if a formal program is not required?

4. What factors are included by Kissner when discussing the human resources planning process? What recruitment decisions are necessary?

5. What is the purpose of the selection process according to Mike Kissner? What comparisons are being made during the process?

6. What factors are considered by Mike Kissner in determining a job candidate's initial pay?

7. What is Susie Christy, manager of employee relations for the Exploration and Production Division of Sun Company, referring to when she discusses melding expectations into one set of goals during the orientation process?

8. What are the three steps in the orientation process for Sun Company noted by Susie Christy?

9. What reason is given by Christy for utilizing the third step in the orientation program?

10. What does Christy include in the third step of the orientation program?

11. What does Susie Christy cite as the purpose of training at Sun Exploration and Production?

12. How are training programs developed according to Susie Christy? What types of training are done at Sun Company?

13. What three goals for performance appraisal are noted by Professor Robert Luke of George Washington University?

14. What is the specific goal of performance appraisal at Sun Exploration according to Christy? What are managers encouraged to do during the year?

15. What specific uses for performance appraisal information are noted by Professor Luke?

16. How is the information from performance appraisals used at Sun Company according to Susie Christy?

**View the television program "Human Resources: Acquisition and Development."**

# After Viewing

— Review and answer the Television Focus Questions. If you are uncertain of the information, or missed a point, view or listen to the program again.

— Review the Key Terms from your text and be sure you understand the Learning Objectives for this lesson.

— Take the Self-Test to check your understanding of the concepts presented in this lesson. Compare your answers to the Answer Key located at the end of the lesson. If you answered incorrectly, the key provides a reference point so you can review the material.

— Extend your learning by completing the Business in Action and Your Business Portfolio sections of the lesson.

## Self-Test

### True/False

**T    F    1.** For an organization to survive and prosper it must be able to identify, select, develop, and retain qualified personnel.

**T    F    2.** Equal Employment Opportunity legislation is designed to provide an employment environment in which job applicants are free from discrimination in their pursuit of employment opportunities.

**T    F    3.** The major factors to be considered in predicting the organization's future demand for people and jobs are technology and the employment history of the company.

**T    F    4.** Selection involves attempts by the organization to identify and attract candidates to meet the requirements of anticipated or actual job openings.

**T    F    5.** According to Susie Christy, manager of employee relations for the Exploration and Production Division of Sun Company, orientation should completely divide the expectations of the company and the employee.

**T    F    6.** A subjective performance appraisal is based on the personal viewpoint of the manager.

**T    F    7.** Fringe benefits are financial rewards provided for employees.

### Multiple Choice

**1.** Which of the following is *not* an element of human resources management?
   **a.** human resources planning
   **b.** orientation
   **c.** motivating
   **d.** training

**2.** Which of the following is an external source of applicants?
   **a.** position vacancies in company newsletters
   **b.** performance records of present employees
   **c.** referrals by relatives
   **d.** advertisements in newspapers

**3.** Which of the following is the step in the selection process in which a person's ability to follow instructions and command of the language are demonstrated?
   **a.** application blank
   **b.** preliminary interview

    **c.** in-depth interviews

    **d.** reference checks

4. Which of the following is a type of training in which the individual learns in a simulated work environment?

    **a.** classical training

    **b.** situational training

    **c.** classroom training

    **d.** vestibule training

5. According to Susie Christy, which of the following is the specific goal of performance appraisal at Sun Company?

    **a.** document the worker

    **b.** improve the performance of the individual

    **c.** take corrective action

    **d.** threaten job security

6. A compensation element that provides incentive money to employees in addition to their regular compensation is

    **a.** a pension plan.

    **b.** a bonus.

    **c.** paid vacations.

    **d.** a stock option.

7. Which of the following is classified as a fringe benefit?

    **a.** child care

    **b.** profit sharing

    **c.** pension plan

    **d.** stock option

# Business in Action

This exercise is designed to have you investigate human resources management as practiced by organizations.

**Step 1.** Interview a human resources manager or personnel manager for a medium or large business. In the interview determine from the manager:

— What activities make up the human resources area of the organization.

— What legislation influences the human resources process.

— What factors are considered in human resources planning.

— From what sources they recruit and what methods are used.

— What steps compose the company's selection process and what is the purpose of each step.

— What type of orientation program the company has, how long it takes, and what elements are included.

— What type of training is provided for employees and what is the purpose of each type.
— What type of performance appraisal system is used and what is its objective.
— What type of employee compensation programs are provided by the company.

**Step 2.** Record the answers to these questions.

**Step 3.** Analyze and compare the interview answers to the material in this lesson.

**Step 4.** Summarize your findings noting differences and similarities between theory and practice.

## Your Business Portfolio

This exercise is designed to have you apply the human resource process.

**Step 1.** Identify a job you once held or presently occupy. For this job:

— List the sources you would utilize for job applicants.
— Describe the methods you would use to attract job applicants.
— Develop a selection process for your job.
— Develop an orientation program, noting the critical areas to be included.
— Identify the kinds of training needed for your job and the type of training method to be used.
— Describe the type of performance appraisal system you would choose and specifically what it would evaluate.

**Step 2.** For each part in Step 1 explain your choices.

**Step 3.** Compare your system to the system employed by the company, noting the differences and similarities.

**Step 4.** Summarize your findings.

## Answer Key

The Answer Key provides a reference for each question: T (text page), TG (Telecourse Guide page), or V (video program).

## True/False

1. **T** (T 136, TG 58)
2. **T** (T 139, TG 58)
3. **F** (T 141)
4. **F** (T 144, TG 58)
5. **F** (V)
6. **T** (T 155)
7. **F** (T 162, TG 59)

## Multiple Choice

1. **c** (T 137, TG 58)
2. **d** (T 144)
3. **a** (T 145)
4. **d** (T 153, V)
5. **b** (V)
6. **b** (T 161)
7. **a** (T 162)

# Lesson

# Managing Human Resources

## Learning Objectives

After studying this lesson, you should be able to:

1. Explain the importance of, and the manager's role in, developing a positive work environment.
2. Explain the influence of Theory X and Theory Y on leadership, motivation, and the work environment.
3. Explain the importance of managers' recognizing individual differences and needs and their influence on motivation.
4. Summarize the motivational theories of Maslow and Herzberg and explain the implications of each on employee motivation.
5. Describe the effect of leadership on employee motivation.
6. Identify and explain the three factors that influence the choice of leadership style.
7. Describe the three major styles of leadership.
8. Discuss the concept of morale and its effect on quality and quantity of work.
9. Describe techniques managers can use to improve the work environment, increase motivation, and improve morale.

## Overview

When an organization has acquired the best possible human resources to perform a job, is there a key ingredient to making them productive and motivated? The answer to that question is a resounding, "Yes!" The challenge for management is to develop a positive work environment where employees can grow and their talents can be utilized. When employees know what is expected of them, that they are appreciated, that all people are treated equitably, that trust exists, and that motivational needs are supported, they can function comfortably. The key to developing this environment or climate is the manager.

The foundation for creating the work environment is a manager's philosophy of management. This is the manager's attitude or beliefs about work and the people who perform the work. The philosophy, in turn, influences leadership style, motivational approach, and ultimately the organizational environment. There are two sets of assumptions—Theory X and Theory Y—that serve as the basis for a manager's approach to working with people. Theory X is a negative philosophy of work, while Theory Y is a positive philosophy.

Another key ingredient in managing human resources and creating a positive organizational environment is the recognition of people as individuals and the need to work with them as individuals. There is no established formula for managing people. All people are different—each person has individual needs, perceptions, values, strengths, and weaknesses. It is up to the manager to recognize these and work with them.

Once a manager has committed to working with people as individuals, there are some tools or theories that can be utilized to understand people. One tool is Maslow's hierarchy of needs theory. It views people as having five universal needs arranged in a sequence, or hierarchy. Each need must be generally satisfied before the person attempts to fill the needs on the next level. The five needs in the order of their priority are physiological, safety and security, social, esteem, and self-actualization. Managers can use this tool to identify workers' needs and to provide an environment in which needs can be satisfied.

A second tool is Herzberg's motivation-maintenance model. This model provides managers two sets of factors that influence how people function in organizations. The presence or absence of these factors influences the organizational climate and, ultimately, motivation. The first set of factors, maintenance or hygiene factors, are those job factors that prevent dissatisfaction but do not generate satisfaction or motivate workers to greater effort. The second set, motivation factors, are factors that provide satisfaction and therefore motivation, but whose absence causes no satisfaction to be achieved.

Using these tools to understand people and the work setting, managers can then provide leadership for the employees and build a comfortable work environment. Leadership is the process of influencing a group or individual to set or achieve a goal. There is no one correct way to lead. Leadership is situational. It is determined by the relationship of the leader, the subordinates, and the work environment.

Based on the leadership situation, managers use different leadership styles. There are three basic options for managers to select from: autocratic, participative, or free-rein. Each has its strengths when applied correctly to a situation. No one style is best; it depends on the situation.

A measure of the quality of leadership provided and of the overall work environment is the morale, or the attitude workers have toward the quality of their total work life. Morale is important because the workers' attitudes toward the quality of work life affect the quality and quantity of output.

**67**

What can managers do to improve the work environment and ultimately increase motivation and improve morale? Managers have a number of techniques or practices they can use in addition to a philosophy, recognition of individual differences, needs provision, and leadership style modification. The approaches can be placed in three categories:

- Management techniques and practices—praise and recognition, delegation, participative management, management by objectives (MBO), quality circles, and the application of people principles.
- Techniques focused on job redesign—job enlargement, job rotation, job enrichment.
- Techniques that provide work flexibility—flextime, job sharing or twinning, and four-day workweek.

## Before Viewing

- Review the Overview and Learning Objectives for this lesson.
- Read the following assignment from the text *before* watching the television segment:
  Straub and Attner, *Introduction to Business,* Third Edition,
  Chapter 7, pages 170–200.
- Define the Key Terms listed in the next section.
- Review the Television Focus Questions and take notes on the questions when viewing the program.

## Key Terms

Terms are referenced to a page of the text.

**autocratic leadership style** (p. 185)
**esteem need** (p. 178)
**exception principle** (p. 195)
**flextime *or* flexible working hours** (p. 197)
**free-rein *or* laissez-faire leadership style** (p. 186)
**job enlargement** (p. 196)
**job enrichment** (p. 196)
**job rotation** (p. 196)
**job sharing *or* twinning** (p. 197)
**leadership** (p. 184)
**leadership style** (p. 185)
**maintenance *or* hygiene factors** (p. 182)
**management by objectives (MBO)** (p. 193)

**morale** (p. 187)
**motivation** (p. 176)
**motivation factors** (p. 182)
**needs** (p. 176)
**participative leadership style** (p. 185)
**philosophy of management** (p. 174)
**physiological need** (p. 177)
**quality circle** (p. 194)
**safety and security need** (p. 178)
**self-actualization *or* self-realization need** (p. 179)
**social need** (p. 178)
**Theory X** (p. 174)
**Theory Y** (p. 174)

## Television Focus Questions

1. How does a manager go about influencing employee performance according to Professor George Labovitz of Boston University? How do you change an employee's behavior?

2. What reasons are given by Don Lawhorne, president of Captronics, for treating people as individuals?

3. What are Maslow's five need levels as noted by Professor Labovitz? What two distinctions does he make in classifying the needs?

4. According to Professor Labovitz, what does the presence of "hygiene factors" ensure?

5. How is Maslow's hierarchy of needs implemented by Lawhorne? How is Herzberg's theory utilized?

6. How is leadership defined by Professor Labovitz? What styles of leadership does he identify?

7. What styles of leadership are utilized by Lawhorne? What examples are provided to illustrate each style?

8. What point is made by Professor Labovitz regarding the best style of leadership?

9. What is the starting point cited by Jim Treybig, president of Tandem Computers, in creating a positive work environment? What else is a key to creating the environment?

10. What is the essence of Tandem's management philosophy noted by Jim Treybig?

11. What is the importance of participation in creating a work environment according to Professor Labovitz? What example does he provide to illustrate the value of participation?

12. What is the value of delegation for the individuals involved as noted by Professor Labovitz?

13. Why does Professor Labovitz consider quality circles a management technique for improving the work environment?

14. How does management by objectives lead to participation according to Professor Labovitz?

15. What is the difference noted by Professor Labovitz between job enlargement and job enrichment?

**View the television program "Managing Human Resources."**

## After Viewing

— Review and answer the Television Focus Questions. If you are uncertain of the information, or missed a point, view or listen to the program again. **69**

- Review the Key Terms from your text and be sure you understand the Learning Objectives for this lesson.
- Take the Self-Test to check your understanding of the concepts presented in this lesson. Compare your answers to the Answer Key located at the end of the lesson. If you answered incorrectly, the key provides a reference point so you can review the material.
- Extend your learning by completing the Business in Action and Your Business Portfolio sections of the lesson.

## Self-Test

### True/False

**T   F   1.** The work environment is a key to developing and maintaining motivated workers.

**T   F   2.** Theory X managers see workers as self-directing and working well independently.

**T   F   3.** According to Don Lawhorne, president of Captronics, individuals in the electronics field have similar experiences and values and can be treated identically.

**T   F   4.** Needs can be strong motivators in the work environment when there is a way, provided by management, to satisfy these needs.

**T   F   5.** According to Professor George Labovitz of Boston University, leadership is based on personality traits of the leader.

**T   F   6.** The autocratic leadership style is appropriate for dealing with crises, short deadlines, new trainees, and less motivated workers.

**T   F   7.** Morale is a measurement of the quality of the work environment.

### Multiple Choice

1. Which of the following is a key point in managing people?
   a. All people should be treated as individuals.
   b. All people want to be treated as a group.
   c. Management of people is difficult.
   d. People avoid responsibility.

2. Which of the following is one of Maslow's identified need levels?
   a. psychological need
   b. physiological need

    c. maintenance need
    d. motivation need

3. According to Professor Labovitz of Boston University, managers have discovered that employees have
    a. freedom needs.
    b. creative needs.
    c. belly and brain needs.
    d. needs for security that overshadow all other needs.

4. Which of the following is considered a maintenance factor?
    a. recognition
    b. achievement
    c. working conditions
    d. advancement

5. A leadership style in which a leader permits the subordinates to function independently is known as
    a. irresponsible.
    b. participative.
    c. free-rein.
    d. supportive.

6. According to Don Lawhorne, president of Captronics, he utilizes a laissez-faire or free-rein style of leadership
    a. in all management situations.
    b. when taking corrective action.
    c. in providing flexibility for individual decision making.
    d. when employees determine their work hours.

7. Which of the following is a job redesign technique of assigning people different jobs or different tasks on a temporary basis?
    a. job enlargement
    b. job rotation
    c. job enrichment
    d. job creation

# Business in Action

This exercise is designed to assist you in investigating leadership styles.

**Step 1.** Interview a manager of a public utility or local government in your community, seeking answers to the following questions:

- What decisions do you make personally?
- How do you involve your subordinates in decision making?
- What decisions are made by your subordinates?

— Do you consider yourself an autocratic, participative, or free-rein leader? Give examples.

— Do you find it necessary to adjust your leadership style? Why?

**Step 2.** Interview a manager of a rapidly growing business in your community and obtain answers to the questions in Step 1. Record the answers to the questions in both interviews.

**Step 3.** Summarize the results of your interviews and compare the differences and similarities of the information from each interview.

## Your Business Portfolio

This exercise is designed for you to evaluate the work environment of your company.

**Step 1.** Read the following statements describing the work environment of your company.

**Step 2.** Rate your environment by placing a number next to each statement, using a scale of 1 (low) to 10 (high). Explain the reason for each rating.

*Rating*

_____ 1. The wages I receive are satisfactory.

_____ 2. My working conditions are satisfactory.

_____ 3. The supervision I receive on the job is satisfactory.

_____ 4. My professional relationship with my superior is satisfactory.

_____ 5. My interpersonal relationship with my superior is satisfactory.

_____ 6. The work I do provides me with satisfaction.

_____ 7. The work I do provides recognition.

_____ 8. The work I do provides opportunities for growth.

_____ 9. The work I do provides a chance for advancement.

_____ 10. The work I do provides opportunity for additional responsibility.

_____ 11. The work I do provides opportunity for achievement.

**Step 3.** Add up your score and compare:

| | |
|---|---|
| 0–40 | You've got trouble. |
| 41–65 | There's hope. |
| 66–85 | That's more like it. |
| 86–100 | Is there an opening? |

# Answer Key

The Answer Key provides a reference for each question: T (text page), TG (Tele-course Guide page), or V (video program).

## True/False

1. **T** (T 173, TG 66, V)
2. **F** (T 174, V)
3. **F** (V)
4. **T** (T 176)
5. **F** (V)
6. **T** (T 185)
7. **T** (T 187, TG 67)

## Multiple Choice

1. **a** (T 175, TG 67, V)
2. **b** (T 177, TG 67, V)
3. **c** (V)
4. **c** (T 182, V)
5. **c** (T 186)
6. **c** (V)
7. **b** (T 196)

# Lesson

# Producing the Product

## Learning Objectives

After studying this lesson, you should be able to:

1. Explain the purpose of the production function in a business.
2. Distinguish between analytic and synthetic production processes.
3. Distinguish between continuous and intermittent production processes.
4. Explain the elements involved in location, design, and layout of production facilities.
5. Relate the functions of inventory control and purchasing to the production function.
6. Identify and explain the elements involved in production control.

## Overview

This lesson is the first of eleven that will start you on a journey through the functions or activities of a business—what actually happens in a business in order to make a profit.

The purpose of the production function of a business is to convert materials and parts into finished products for the company to market. In doing this it utilizes machinery and people to create the finished product. What is the total production management picture?

When looked at in totality the production function and production management involve more than producing a product. Production management should be involved in the decision on what products are to be produced. This decision then sets in motion plans for the physical location of the facility. In turn, the production facility must be designed and laid out, materials and equipment purchased, and employees hired and trained. Finally, production includes the development of a system to coordinate people, materials, and machinery (production control).

Once the decision is made regarding what product to produce, the production function logically develops. Where does the plant need to be located to produce the product effectively and efficiently? The location decision is made by carefully evaluating three factors: proximity factors, people factors, and physical factors.

The type of product also determines what production processes will be used to produce the product. The initial production process decision focuses on what means will be used or what will be done to the raw materials (analytic or synthetic process). The second element of the process is how the processes are performed over time (intermittent or continuous process).

The product to be produced and the processes performed to produce the product dictate the design and layout of the facility. There are two primary layout alternatives: process and product. A process layout is used in intermittent production. It is designed to accommodate a wide variety of nonstandard products that are produced in relatively small amounts. In this type of layout the material is moved in batches to the operators by variable path equipment (for example, forklifts, hand trucks, dollies). A product layout is often referred to as a flow, continuous, or line layout. It is designed to accommodate one or very few product designs. In this type of layout the material is moved continuously in a flow to the operator by fixed path equipment (assembly lines, conveyor belts).

With the actual layout of the production facility developed, the next question is how to ensure the smooth flow of material to make the product. This concern falls into the area of materials management. This involves not only the actual purchasing of the materials, but also decisions on the type of purchasing to be done (hand-to-mouth, forward, anticipatory) as well as decisions on suppliers (single source, bid, or contract purchasing). A second area of materials management focuses on inventory control. What will be the policy of the company on inventory levels? Will the company maintain inventory of all component parts and raw materials—or one or the other? In addition, what role will the vendor play to facilitate limited inventory levels?

When all these production decisions are made, a system needs to be developed to coordinate the interaction of people, materials, and machinery so that products are made in the proper amounts at the required times to fill orders. This is the area of production control. It involves the steps of production planning, routing, scheduling, dispatching, follow-up, and quality assurance. Each one is vital to the final production of a product.

## Before Viewing

— Review the Overview and Learning Objectives for this lesson.
— Read the following assignment from the text *before* watching the television segment:

Straub and Attner, *Introduction to Business*, Third Edition, Chapter 9, pages 240–268.

— Define the Key Terms listed in the next section.

— Review the Television Focus Questions and take notes on the questions when viewing the program.

## Key Terms

Terms are referenced to a page of the text.

analytic process  (p. 251)
anticipatory purchasing  (p. 258)
assembly process  (p. 251)
bid purchasing  (p. 259)
captive supplier  (p. 259)
continuous process  (p. 253)
contract purchasing  (p. 259)
dispatching  (p. 264)
economic order quantity (EOQ)
   (p. 262)
environmental impact study
   (p. 247)
fabrication process  (p. 251)
follow-up  (p. 264)
forward purchasing  (p. 258)
hand-to-mouth purchasing  (p. 258)
intermittent process  (p. 253)
inventory control  (p. 261)
job shops  (p. 253)
lead time  (p. 262)

make versus buy *or* in-house versus
   out-of-house  (p. 259)
manufacturing company  (p. 243)
motion study  (p. 250)
on-site inspection  (p. 257)
processing company  (p. 243)
production  (p. 243)
production control  (p. 262)
production management  (p. 244)
production plan  (p. 263)
purchasing agent  (p. 256)
purchasing procedure  (p. 256)
quality assurance  (p. 265)
robot  (p. 254)
routing  (p. 263)
scheduling  (p. 264)
single-source purchasing  (p. 259)
synthetic process  (p. 251)
time study  (p. 250)

## Television Focus Questions

1. How does Professor John Carlson of the University of Southern California define production?

2. What activities does Professor Carlson note are included in production? What specific decisions are included in the activities?

3. How does Professor Carlson describe the analytic and synthetic processes of production?

4. What production options does Professor Carlson identify? When is each type of production most applicable?

5. What type of layout and equipment does Professor Carlson state are identified with a continuous production operation? An intermittent production operation?

6. What does Professor Carlson note determines the type of production lay-out?

7. What does Production Operations Manager John Otterstedt cite as the production objectives at Apple's Macintosh plant?

8. How did the objective dictate the use of a continuous production system according to John Livingston, management information system manager at Apple's Macintosh plant?

9. What does John Livingston note as considerations in the layout of the facilities?

10. How do Otterstedt and Livingston describe the relationship of the assembly operators to the flow of materials in the assembling process?

11. What does Dale Larson, vice-president and general manager, cite as the production objective at Typco Graphics? How do customer needs influence products?

12. What does Larson state is the impact of the needs of customers on the time of a job, the equipment, the employees, and the production layout?

13. What activities does Professor Carlson include in production control? What is involved in each activity?

14. What does Professor Carlson note is the role of quality control?

**View the television program "Producing the Product."**


# After Viewing

— Review and answer the Television Focus Questions. If you are uncertain of the information, or missed a point, view or listen to the program again.

— Review the Key Terms from your text and be sure you understand the Learning Objectives for this lesson.

— Take the Self-Test to check your understanding of the concepts presented in this lesson. Compare your answers to the Answer Key located at the end of the lesson. If you answered incorrectly, the key provides a reference point so you can review the material.

— Extend your learning by completing the Business in Action and Your Business Portfolio sections of the lesson.


# Self-Test

## True/False

T    F    1. Production is the business activity or function responsible for converting materials and parts into products for the company to market.

**T  F  2.** Choosing a plant site requires careful thought and investigation.

**T  F  3.** In the analytic process raw material is broken down to form new products.

**T  F  4.** According to Dale Larson, vice-president and general manager of Typco Graphics, the nature of their product dictates that a continuous process be used.

**T  F  5.** An approach to purchasing that specifies a relatively large quantity to fill needs over long periods of time is known as forward purchasing.

**T  F  6.** Inventory control balances the need for adequate stock against the costs of purchasing, handling, storing, and keeping records on the stock.

**T  F  7.** The area of production control includes only quality assurance for a product.

## Multiple Choice

1. Which of the following is *not* included as an element in the total production management picture?
   a. plant location decisions
   b. plant layout decisions
   c. determining consumer needs
   d. coordinating people, resources, and machinery

2. Which of the following is one of the factors that needs to be considered in a plant location decision?
   a. advertising costs
   b. accounting procedures
   c. banking capabilities
   d. proximity factors

3. According to Professor John Carlson of the University of Southern California, the analytic process is associated with
   a. producing automobiles.
   b. creating television sets.
   c. the production of oil.
   d. building refrigerators.

4. An intermittent production process is used by a company that
   a. creates an identical product each time.
   b. manufactures automobiles on an assembly line.
   c. readjusts operations to make a slightly different product.
   d. does none of the above.

5. Which of the following is an element of materials management?
   a. designing the production control system
   b. identifying potential suppliers

c. creating engineering drawings
d. moving the completed product to the shipping dock

6. Which of the following is a potential layout alternative for a production facility?
   a. inverted layout
   b. promotional layout
   c. circular layout
   d. product layout

7. The step in production control that allots the time for each production step along the route is known as
   a. routing.
   b. scheduling.
   c. dispatching.
   d. follow-up.

# Business in Action

This exercise is designed to have you investigate the production function of business.

**Step 1.** Identify a meat market or a grocery store with a meat market incorporated in it.

**Step 2.** Interview the manager of the meat market or meat department in the grocery store using the following questions:

— Production Processes
   a. When the raw materials (beef, poultry, pork, lamb) are delivered what form are they in (i.e., sides of beef, whole chickens)?
   b. What final products are produced from these raw materials?
   c. What steps are involved in producing the final products from these raw materials?
   d. What equipment is required to prepare the products from the time they are received until the consumer selects them?
   e. Do you use the same equipment for different products? If so, what adjustments need to be made to the equipment?
   f. Why has the equipment used in the processes been located in their particular places?

— Materials Management
   a. Who do you purchase your materials from?
   b. How many suppliers do you use?
   c. How often do you order and for what period of time?

— Production Control
   a. How do you plan what products are to be produced (i.e., steak, hamburger, roasts)?

    **b.** How do you determine when the products will be produced and in what order?

    **c.** How do you ensure the quality of your products?

**Step 3.** Identify a car or van customizing business, a hamburger fast-food restaurant, or furniture upholstery shop.

**Step 4.** Interview the owner or manager using the questions in Step 2.

**Step 5.** Record the answers to each question.

**Step 6.** Summarize and discuss your findings. In each case identify both the means of manufacturing involved (analytic or synthetic) and how the processes are performed over time (continuous or intermittent).

## Your Business Portfolio

This exercise is designed to involve you in the production function.

**Step 1.** Select from the following list a product to manufacture in your home: pizza, chocolate chip cookies, omelettes, or homemade bread.

**Step 2.** Produce the product you selected and answer these questions:

— Production Processes
    **a.** Was the process involved analytic or synthetic? Why?
    **b.** To manufacture this product for sale would you recommend a continuous or intermittent process? Why?
    **c.** What distinct production steps were involved?
    **d.** What equipment was required?
    **e.** How did you lay out your production facilities to produce the product?

— Materials Management
    **a.** Where did you purchase your raw materials?
    **b.** How did you decide to use these vendors?
    **c.** Did you use raw materials from inventory, or did you purchase all the ingredients at the time of production?
    **d.** How would you categorize the purchasing practice in the previous question (i.e., hand-to-mouth)?
    **e.** Did you store your finished good, or was it used immediately?

— Production Control
    **a.** What production planning took place before producing the product?
    **b.** How did you schedule the various activities that took place and route the raw materials to complete the steps?

    c. What quality assurance steps did you build into the process, (i.e., tasting, smelling, timing, viewing)?

**Step 3.** Record and analyze your answers.

**Step 4.** Discuss your findings.

## Answer Key

The Answer Key provides a reference for each question: T (text page), TG (Telecourse Guide page), or V (video program).

### True/False

1. **T** (T 243, TG 74)
2. **T** (T 244)
3. **T** (T 251, V)
4. **F** (V)
5. **T** (T 258)
6. **T** (T 261)
7. **F** (T 262, 263, TG 75)

### Multiple Choice

1. **c** (T 244, TG 74)
2. **d** (T 245, TG 75)
3. **c** (V)
4. **c** (T 253, V)
5. **b** (T 258, TG 75)
6. **d** (TG 75)
7. **b** (T 264)

# Lesson

## 11

# Marketing Concepts

## Learning Objectives

After studying this lesson, you should be able to:

1. Define the term *marketing.*
2. Describe the importance of marketing to a business.
3. List and explain the functions involved in marketing.
4. Describe the evolution of an organization from production orientation to marketing orientation.
5. Explain the marketing concept and its effect on the role of marketing in an organization.
6. Describe the marketing process.
7. Define what a market is and distinguish between industrial and consumer markets.
8. Explain what marketing research is and how it is applied.
9. Explain the process of target marketing and relate it to market segmentation.
10. Describe the four elements of the marketing mix.
11. Relate the marketing mix and target marketing to the development of marketing strategy.

## Overview

This is the first of a five-lesson segment examining the marketing function in a business. The purpose of the lesson is to examine the critical elements of marketing and to identify the four components of marketing strategy. Each of the four remaining lessons in the block of marketing lessons will explore one of the areas in marketing strategy.

What is marketing? Is marketing really selling with a "fancy name"? The answer to this question is that marketing includes selling and much, much more. Marketing is a group of interrelated activities designed to identify consumer needs and to develop, distribute, promote, and price goods and services to satisfy these needs at a profit.

Marketing and the practice of marketing are critical to the success of modern organizations. Companies can no longer approach the marketplace with the idea that the consumer will buy a product simply because the company has one for sale. Consumers want *their* needs satisfied from *their* point of view, not the company's point of view. Companies that do not practice sound marketing will face a difficult future in the marketplace.

Businesses did not always approach the consumer from a marketing point of view. Companies have gone through a series of changes from production orientation to sales orientation and finally to a marketing orientation. In the process of this transition companies that have arrived at the marketing orientation stage have adopted the marketing concept as a guideline. Simply stated, the marketing concept is a belief that the company should adopt a companywide consumer orientation directed at long-range profitability.

When companies practice marketing they utilize a process that includes identifying and analyzing a potential target market of consumers and developing a unique marketing mix to reach the target market. In completing this overall process a number of marketing activities take place. These activities, referred to as marketing functions, fall into three major categories: exchange functions (buying and selling), physical distribution functions (transporting and storing), and facilitating functions (financing, risk bearing, obtaining market information, and standardizing and grading).

The starting point of marketing is to identify a potential target market of consumers. A market is a group of potential customers with the authority and the ability to purchase a particular product or service that satisfies their collective demand. There are two general markets for products and services: the consumer market and the industrial market. These markets have been categorized by who buys the products and for what purpose the purchase is intended.

For a marketer to successfully market, these markets need to be more specific than simply consumer or industrial markets. Marketers further divide a total market into subgroups or distinct target markets by practicing market segmentation. Through extensive marketing research marketers are able to analyze the needs of the particular market segment or target market. In addition, they are able to research the potential of the target market for demand, sales, buying power, and profit potential.

Once the target market has been identified, the marketer must develop an overall plan to reach it. The tools, or variables, a marketer works with are product strategy, promotion strategy, price strategy, and distribution strategy. The meshing of these is known as the marketing mix.

## Before Viewing

— Review the Overview and Learning Objectives for this lesson.
— Read the following assignment from the text *before* watching the television segment:
Straub and Attner, *Introduction to Business*, Third Edition, Chapter 10, pages 272–286.
— Define the Key Terms listed in the next section.
— Review the Television Focus Questions and take notes on the questions when viewing the program.

## Key Terms

Terms are referenced to a page of the text.

consumer market (p. 282)
exchange functions (p. 277)
facilitating functions (p. 278)
industrial market (p. 282)
market (p. 281)
marketing (p. 274)
marketing concept (p. 276)
marketing mix (p. 285)
marketing orientation (p. 276)

marketing research (p. 279)
market segmentation (p. 282)
physical distribution functions (p. 278)
production orientation (p. 276)
retailers (p. 278)
sales orientation (p. 276)
wholesalers (p. 278)

## Television Focus Questions

1. What is the specific emphasis of production orientation, sales orientation, and marketing orientation according to Professor William Stanton of the University of Colorado?
2. What does Professor Stanton cite as the impact on modern business of the marketing evolution?
3. What activities or functions does Professor Stanton identify that take place in marketing?
4. What is a company actually doing when it markets according to Professor Stanton? What are the elements of the marketing mix?
5. What does Professor Stanton note is involved in segmenting a target market from an overall market? What three bases of marketing segmentation may be used?
6. What specific reason is given by Professor Stanton for forecasting the sales potential of an identified market segment?
7. After establishing goals for the whole marketing organization, what seven elements does Professor Stanton include in explaining the marketing process?

8. What was the initial target market identified by Earl Shirley, product manager for the Tortilla Chips Division of Frito-Lay, Inc., for Sabritos Tortilla Chips? What type of research was done? What were the results of the research?

9. What does Earl Shirley describe as the specific target market for Sabritos Tortilla Chips?

10. What does Earl Shirley identify as the needs of the target market?

11. What is the potential of the target market according to Earl Shirley?

12. How did Frito-Lay develop a product to satisfy the consumer needs according to Earl Shirley?

13. What does Shirley state is the price strategy for Sabritos? Why?

14. What is the distribution strategy for Sabritos? Why?

15. What does Earl Shirley describe as the promotion strategy for Sabritos? Why?

16. What reasons are given by Earl Shirley for deciding on this particular marketing mix?

**View the television program "Marketing Concepts."**

# After Viewing

— Review and answer the Television Focus Questions. If you are uncertain of the information, or missed a point, view or listen to the program again.

— Review the Key Terms from your text and be sure you understand the Learning Objectives for this lesson.

— Take the Self-Test to check your understanding of the concepts presented in this lesson. Compare your answers to the Answer Key located at the end of the lesson. If you answered incorrectly, the key provides a reference point so you can review the material.

— Extend your learning by completing the Business in Action and Your Business Portfolio sections of the lesson.

# Self-Test

## True/False

T F 1. Marketing can best be described with this statement: "build a better mousetrap and the world will beat a path to your door."

T F 2. The Model T Ford developed by Henry Ford is an excellent example of marketing orientation.

T   F   3. According to Professor William Stanton of the University of Colorado, the marketing functions or activities include pricing, promoting, and distributing.

T   F   4. A market is defined as a group of potential customers.

T   F   5. According to Earl Shirley, product manager for the Tortilla Chips Division of Frito-Lay, Inc., Sabritos were developed by the marketing department with minimal research.

T   F   6. Market segmentation refers simply to the identification of consumer and industrial markets.

T   F   7. Pricing strategy is influenced by how responsive a target market is to a high or low price.

## Multiple Choice

1. Marketing includes which of the following?
   a. product development
   b. consumer behavior
   c. promotion
   d. all of the above

2. According to Professor William Stanton of the University of Colorado, for the modern corporation marketing is
   a. considered as a minimum investment.
   b. equated with selling.
   c. recognized as the key to success.
   d. a contributor to profits.

3. Which of the following is a use of accurate marketing research data?
   a. aids in writing promotional messages
   b. aids in firing employees
   c. aids in acquiring finances
   d. aids in reprogramming research models

4. Which of the following is an element or step in the marketing process?
   a. Identify the resources of the company.
   b. Mobilize the resources of the company.
   c. Warranty products of the company.
   d. Ensure satisfaction through after-sales service.

5. Which of the following is a category of a market?
   a. institutional market
   b. industrial market
   c. individual market
   d. incidental market

6. Which of the following is a type of market segmentation?
   a. structural segmentation
   b. unilateral segmentation

c. benefit segmentation
d. personal segmentation
7. According to Earl Shirley, product manager for the Tortilla Chips Division of Frito-Lay, Inc., the marketing mix for Sabritos Tortilla Chips was selected because of
a. the need for trade support and price factors.
b. the taste of the product and the package.
c. the promotional plan necessary.
d. the quality of the product.

## Business in Action

This exercise is designed to have you investigate the marketing process.

**Step 1.** Identify either a men's clothing store or a women's clothing store with multiple locations.

**Step 2.** Interview either the owner or a top manager in the organization and ask the following questions:

— Who is your target market customer?
a. What is the average age?
b. What is the income bracket?
c. Where does the person live?
d. What educational background does the person appear to have?
e. What are the person's interests?
f. Why does the person purchase clothing here?

— What products have you chosen to satisfy this target market?
a. Why did you select this particular product or products?
b. How does the target market perceive this product?

— What promotion strategy have you used to reach the target market?
a. What advertising have you used?
b. How important is personal selling?
c. Have you used any promotional events?

— What pricing strategy have you chosen to use for this target market?
a. How do the prices you charge relate to product image?
b. What discounts, sales, or specials, if any, are used?

— What distribution strategy have you used to reach the target market?
a. How many stores do you have?
b. How did you determine the number of stores to use?
c. How did you decide to operate the stores in their present locations? **87**

**Step 3.** Record and analyze your answers.

**Step 4.** Discuss your observations.

## Your Business Portfolio

This exercise is designed to involve you in target marketing.

**Step 1.** Select a restaurant in your city (not a fast-food restaurant).

**Step 2.** Eat at the restaurant during a peak time period at night.

**Step 3.** Answer the following questions:

— Demographic Segmentation
- **a.** What is the average age of the customers?
- **b.** What is the family profile (single, couple, two adults—two children)?
- **c.** What is the income bracket?

— Psychographic Segmentation
- **a.** What appear to be the career activities of the customers?
- **b.** What appear to be their interests (recreation)?
- **c.** What appears to be their life-style?

— Geographic Segmentation
- **a.** How far from the restaurant do the patrons live? (Ask the manager the size of the trade radius.)
- **b.** Are the patrons located in a specific section of the trade radius?

— Benefit Segmentation
- **a.** What is the quality of the food?
- **b.** What is the price/quality relationship?
- **c.** What is the public image of the restaurant?
- **d.** What entertainment is provided by the restaurant?

**Step 4.** Summarize and discuss your analysis of the market segment targeted by the restaurant.

## Answer Key

The Answer Key provides a reference for each question: T (text page), TG (Telecourse Guide page), or V (video program).

## True/False

1. **F** (T 274)
2. **F** (T 276)
3. **F** (V)
4. **F** (T 281, TG 83, V)
5. **F** (V)
6. **F** (T 282, TG 83, V)
7. **T** (T 285, 286)

## Multiple Choice

1. **d** (T 274)
2. **c** ((V)
3. **a** (T 279)
4. **d** (T 280, 281, V)
5. **b** (T 282, TG 83, V)
6. **c** (T 284, V)
7. **a** (V)

# Lesson

## 12

# Marketing Product Strategy

## Learning Objectives

After studying this lesson, you should be able to:

1. Describe the importance of the product and product strategy in marketing strategy.
2. Describe the tangible and intangible components of a product.
3. Distinguish between consumer and industrial products.
4. Describe the four stages of the life cycle of a product.
5. Relate the importance of new product development to the life cycle of the product.
6. Explain the importance of brands and packaging as elements of product strategy.

## Overview

In marketing the identification of consumer needs leads to the creation of a product or service to satisfy these needs. In turn, the product and the product strategy developed by the company serve as the cornerstone in the development of the overall marketing mix.

What is a product? A product is not just what you can see or touch—the tangible features. It also includes the intangible elements—what the product will do (benefits), what it means to own the product (status or image), and what accompanies the product (service, warranties). Both the tangibles and intangibles are what consumers really buy and what marketers focus on in developing product strategy.

Are all products the same? No. Products can be placed in two categories—consumer products and industrial products. Consumer products are intended for the personal use of the consumer and include convenience, shopping, and specialty goods. On the other hand, industrial products are goods or services purchased for the production of other goods or services or to be used in the operation of a business. Industrial goods include installations, accessory equipment, fabricated parts and materials, raw materials, and industrial supplies.

Regardless of whether a product is a consumer product or an industrial product, a company needs to develop a product strategy. A concern of product strategy is developing an image to distinguish the product from others on the market. One approach is to adopt a branding strategy by using a brand name, brand mark, or trademark. Another approach to distinguishing a product from its competitors is the use of shape, color, and material in packaging.

A factor that marketers must remember about products is that unless the product continues to serve a need it will not remain in the marketplace. Products pass through several stages from the time they appear on the market until they disappear. These phases are collectively referred to as the product life cycle. They include introduction, growth, maturity, and decline stages.

The product life cycle is an important tool for a marketer. No one creates a product to see it go off the market. The product life cycle provides a method to monitor the product on the market. It allows the marketer to see the introduction of competition when it occurs and its effect on sales and profit. In turn, the marketer can use this information either to modify the product and the marketing mix or to begin new product development to replace the product.

Regardless of how well a company monitors its product in the marketplace and modifies it to keep it selling, the product eventually moves through all phases of the product life cycle. As a result, it is necessary for companies to have new products planned as replacements for existing ones.

## Before Viewing

— Review the Overview and Learning Objectives for this lesson.
— Read the following assignment from the text *before* watching the television segment:
Straub and Attner, *Introduction to Business*, Third Edition, Chapter 10, pages 286–296.
— Define the Key Terms listed in the next section.
— Review the Television Focus Questions and take notes on the questions when viewing the program.

## Key Terms

Terms are referenced to a page of the text.

**accessory equipment** (p. 288)          **brand name** (p. 288)
**brand** (p. 288)                        **consumer products** (p. 287)
**brand mark** (p. 289)                   **convenience goods** (p. 287)

**fabricated parts and materials**
(p. 288)
**generic products**  (p. 289)
**industrial products**  (p. 288)
**industrial supplies**  (p. 288)
**installations**  (p. 288)
**product life cycle**  (p. 290)

**raw materials**  (p. 288)
**shopping goods**  (p. 287)
**specialty goods**  (p. 287)
**test marketing**  (p. 291)
**trade character**  (p. 289)
**trademark**  (p. 289)

## Television Focus Questions

1. What does Professor William Stanton of the University of Colorado say is the importance of the product in the overall marketing strategy?

2. How does Professor Jerome McCarthy, Michigan State University, describe a product?

3. Why would a marketer need to classify products, in Professor McCarthy's opinion?

4. Why is it important for a marketing manager to understand and monitor a product's life cycle, according to Professor McCarthy?

5. Which elements of the marketing mix does Professor McCarthy say may have to be changed during the product's life cycle?

6. What three factors or elements does Professor Stanton identify that influence the overall product strategy?

7. What element is added to the product strategy by Professor McCarthy?

8. How does Jeff Jones, associate advertising manager of Procter & Gamble, describe Pampers as a product? Why?

9. What does Jones say is the importance of monitoring the life cycle of a product in the marketplace? What example is provided to support this?

10. How does this monitoring process affect the overall marketing strategy according to Jones? What examples are provided to support this?

11. What does Jones state was Pampers' initial product strategy?

12. What does Jones identify as the three elements of Pampers' initial marketing strategy?

13. What modifications does Jones note that were made in product strategy as Pampers moved out of the introductory stage of the product life cycle?

14. What changes did Jones say were made in the overall marketing strategy as a result of changes in the product strategy?

15. What role does Jones say product development plays in the overall marketing strategy?

**View the television program "Marketing Product Strategy."**

# After Viewing

- Review and answer the Television Focus Questions. If you are uncertain of the information, or missed a point, view or listen to the program again.
- Review the Key Terms from your text and be sure you understand the Learning Objectives for this lesson.
- Take the Self-Test to check your understanding of the concepts presented in this lesson. Compare your answers to the Answer Key located at the end of the lesson. If you answered incorrectly, the key provides a reference point so you can review the material.
- Extend your learning by completing the Business in Action and Your Business Portfolio sections of the lesson.

# Self-Test

## True/False

T  F   1. A product has minimal significance in the development of the marketing mix.

T  F   2. A product includes both tangible and intangible features.

T  F   3. Goods intended for personal use are known as conditional goods.

T  F   4. The product life cycle refers to the stages a product passes through from the time it enters the market until it leaves the market.

T  F   5. An example of a brand name is Tony the Tiger.

T  F   6. According to Professor William Stanton of the University of Colorado, the decision on branding is simply and easily made.

T  F   7. Packaging aids in image creation.

## Multiple Choice

1. Which of the following describes a product?
   a. It includes tangible features only.
   b. It includes pricing as an element.
   c. It includes promotion as an element.
   d. It includes physical, image, and service features.
2. Which of the following is a category of products?
   a. institutional product
   b. industrial product

    **c.** individual product

    **d.** educational product

  **3.** A good that is necessary in the daily operation of the firm is

    **a.** an installation.

    **b.** accessory equipment.

    **c.** an industrial supply.

    **d.** a packaged good.

  **4.** Which of the following is a stage in the product life cycle?

    **a.** initiation

    **b.** continuance

    **c.** maturity

    **d.** saturation

  **5.** According to Jeff Jones, associate advertising manager for Procter & Gamble, the product life cycle

    **a.** has minimal impact on product strategy.

    **b.** is a theoretical concept not applicable in industry.

    **c.** results in questionable information.

    **d.** is critical for product strategy.

  **6.** Which of the following is a brand mark that has a human quality?

    **a.** a trade name

    **b.** a brand name

    **c.** a brand mark

    **d.** a trade character

  **7.** Which of the following is an element of packaging strategy?

    **a.** the use of color

    **b.** the use of famous individuals

    **c.** the use of endorsements

    **d.** the use of coupons

## Business in Action

This exercise is designed to acquaint you with the importance of and elements involved in product strategy.

**Step 1.** Identify a company (manufacturer or retailer) that markets a consumer product that interests you.

**Step 2.** Interview the person responsible for developing the product's marketing strategy. During the interview ask the following questions:

  — How would you describe this product from the consumer's perspective?

    **a.** What are the tangible features?

    **b.** What services or benefits are provided to the consumer by the product?

    **c.** What image is a part of the product?

— How do you classify this product (convenience, shopping, or specialty good)?

— What is the target market for the product?

— What are the elements of your product strategy?
   a. What elements of the product have you chosen to market to the consumer?
   b. What is the competition for this product?
   c. How have you chosen to position the product as a result of competition?
   d. What role has packaging played in marketing the product?
   e. What role has branding played in marketing the product?
   f. Is this product part of a product line? If so, what role does this play in the strategy?

— What elements of your marketing strategy have you created to support the product strategy?
   a. What is the distribution strategy?
   b. What is the promotion strategy?
   c. What is the pricing strategy?

**Step 3.** Record the answers to these questions and analyze the responses.

**Step 4.** Discuss your conclusions.

## Your Business Portfolio

This exercise is designed to provide experience with product strategy.

**Step 1.** Select a consumer product that you have in your household from the following list: laundry detergent, cookies, hand soap, coffee, or a soft drink.

**Step 2.** Assume you are the manufacturer of this product and begin to reconstruct the product strategy by answering the following questions:

— What tangible features of the product were communicated to the final consumer through advertising?

— What intangible features of the product were communicated to the final consumer through advertising?
   a. What benefits will the consumer receive?
   b. What image is established?

— What packaging elements are part of the product?
   a. What messages are contained on the packaging?
   b. Does the package have multiple uses?
   c. Is the package designed for safety? Convenience? Appeal?

— Are there multiple sizes of the same product?

— Is the product a brand product?
   a. What branding strategy was used (family, individual)?
   b. Was use made of trademarks, trade characters, or brand names?

**Step 3.** Record the answers to the questions and analyze the results.

**Step 4.** Summarize the product strategy for the product by completing the following elements:

— The product as seen by the consumer is:

— The product features, benefits, and image that will serve as the formulation for the strategy are:

— The packaging strategy for this product will include:

— The branding strategy for the product will include:

## Answer Key

The Answer Key provides a reference for each question: T (text page), TG (Telecourse Guide page), or V (video program).

### True/False

1. F (T 286, TG 90, V)
2. T (T 286, TG 90, V)
3. F (T 287, TG 90, V)
4. T (T 290, TG 91, V)
5. F (T 288, 289)
6. F (V)
7. T (T 290, TG 91)

### Multiple Choice

1. d (T 286, TG 90)
2. b (T 286, TG 90, V)
3. c (T 288)
4. c (T 290, TG 91, V)
5. d (V)
6. d (T 289)
7. a (T 290, TG 91)

# Lesson

# Marketing Promotional Strategy

## Learning Objectives

After studying this lesson, you should be able to:
1. Describe the role and importance of promotion in marketing strategy.
2. Identify the principal buying motives of final consumers and those of industrial buyers.
3. Identify the four elements of the promotional mix and explain how they are combined to form an effective mix for an identified product and market.
4. Identify the eight elements of the communication process.
5. Define personal selling and present the seven steps in the selling process.
6. Define advertising and identify the two types.
7. List and describe the advantages and disadvantages of advertising media.
8. Define publicity and explain its importance.
9. Define sales promotion and describe the sales promotion technique that can be used to appeal to middlemen and final consumers.
10. Identify and explain two promotional strategies.

## Overview

*I wish that I had known Johnson's had that weedeater. I wouldn't have searched all over town.*

*Be sure and place the 'reminder ad' for Valentine's Day in the paper. We wouldn't want all those people getting in trouble with their sweethearts!*

*Hey, hon, did you know it says right here in this ad that if you use gas heating over electricity it saves one-third of your heating bill?*

The comments you have just read would make a marketer smile. Each one focuses on the importance of promotion strategy, the second element in the marketing mix and the topic of this lesson. It is the communication element of the marketing mix and of marketing strategy. Regardless of how outstanding a product or service might be in satisfying a consumer need, the consumer won't buy if the product or its merits are unknown.

To compose promotional messages and ideas that inform, persuade, or remind the consumer, the marketer must understand why consumers buy the items they do; in other words, what makes a final consumer and an industrial buyer buy a product. The "whys" are known as buying motives. There are two categories of motives: consumer and industrial. Consumer buying motives include emotional, rational, and patronage motives. Industrial motives include profit, price, quality, salability, uniformity, service, emotion, and reciprocity.

Once the buying motives of the target have been identified, the marketer creates the promotional strategy. A marketer works with four elements in promotion: personal selling, advertising, publicity, and sales promotion. The blending of these four elements is known as the promotional mix. To develop a proper blending for effective communication, a starting point is to understand the communication process. It consists of eight elements: the sender, encoding, the message, the medium, decoding, the target market, feedback, and noise.

One tool or element of the promotional mix that can be used to communicate messages to the target market is personal selling. It should be utilized when the product or service requires face-to-face communication. When salespersons are involved in persuading potential customers to make purchases, they utilize a seven-step selling process. It includes prospecting, preapproach, approach, presentation, handling objections, closing, and follow-up.

A second tool or element of the promotional mix is advertising. Advertising is intended to inform, persuade, and remind the target market about the products or services. Companies can use two types of advertising: product and institutional. To communicate these messages, marketers have a number of media from which to choose. Each has its strengths and weaknesses. The media include daily newspapers, television, direct mail, magazines, radio, outdoor, and transit.

A third element of the promotional mix is publicity. Companies constantly strive to incorporate publicity in their promotional mixes because it is something they cannot buy. Publicity is nonpaid and nonpersonal communicaton that promotes the products, services, or image of the company. Publicity is given to a company by independent media. To take advantage of this free advertising, companies must work to prepare newsworthy items for the media.

The fourth element of the promotional mix is sales promotion. It is intended to support the other three elements of the marketing mix by stimulating consumer purchasing and dealer effectiveness. Sales promotion can be directed at the middlemen through point-of-purchase displays, cooperative advertising programs, specialty advertising, trade shows, and push money. It can also be directed at final consumers by using coupons, samples, premiums, special services, contests and sweepstakes, trading stamps, and refund offers.

Each of the four promotional elements serves a different function. Ultimately they need to be blended together to form a promotional strategy for a particular product. There are two potential strategies: push strategy and pull strategy. A push strategy is directed at members of the marketing channel; a pull strategy is aimed at the consumer.

## Before Viewing

— Review the Overview and Learning Objectives for this lesson.
— Read the following assignment from the text *before* watching the television segment:
Straub and Attner, *Introduction to Business*, Third Edition, Chapter 11, pages 298–324.
— Define the Key Terms listed in the next section.
— Review the Television Focus Questions and take notes on the questions when viewing each program.

## Key Terms

Terms are referenced to a page of the text.

**advertising** (p. 310)
**advertising media** (p. 311)
**approach** (p. 309)
**close** (p. 310)
**communication process** (p. 306)
**consumer buying motives** (p. 302)
**cooperative advertising programs** (p. 318)
**decoding** (p. 308)
**emotional motives** (p. 302)
**encoding** (p. 307)
**feedback** (p. 308)
**follow-up** (p. 310)
**industrial buying motives** (p. 303)
**institutional advertising** (p. 311)
**medium** (p. 308)
**message** (p. 308)
**noise** (p. 308)
**objections** (p. 309)
**patronage motives** (p. 303)

**personal selling** (p. 308)
**point-of-purchase displays** (p. 317)
**preapproach** (p. 309)
**premium** (p. 320)
**presentation** (p. 309)
**product advertising** (p. 311)
**promotional mix** (p. 306)
**prospecting** (p. 308)
**publicity** (p. 316)
**pull strategy** (p. 321)
**push money ("PMs" *or* "spiffs")** (p. 318)
**push strategy** (p. 321)
**rational motives** (p. 303)
**reciprocal buying** (p. 306)
**sales promotion** (p. 317)
**selling process** (p. 308)
**sender** (p. 307)
**specialty advertising** (p. 318)
**target market** (p. 308)

**99**

## Television Focus Questions

1.  What does Professor Jerry DeHay of Tarleton State University state is the role of promotion?
2.  What does Professor Jerome McCarthy of Michigan State University cite as the objectives of promotional strategy?
3.  What does Professor DeHay include as a purpose of promotion?
4.  According to Professor McCarthy, what promotional tools does a business have?
5.  What does Professor DeHay say is involved in each of the four promotional tools?
6.  How is each of the four tools best utilized according to Professor McCarthy?
7.  What does Professor McCarthy state that a marketing manager must do to utilize the elements effectively?
8.  What specific factors does Professor McCarthy include that influence the use of the four elements? What additional factors are added by Professor DeHay?
9.  What does Earl Shirley, product manager for Tortilla Chips of Frito-Lay, cite as the target market for Doritos?
10. How did the choice of target markets dictate the overall promotional strategy according to Earl Shirley? What does the target market respond to?
11. What does Earl Shirley state is the role of personal selling in the promotional mix for Doritos?
12. What does Earl Shirley note is the role of publicity?
13. What place does Earl Shirley state advertising has in the promotional mix?
14. What does Earl Shirley focus on as the role of sales promotion? What sales promotion devices are included?
15. According to Professor McCarthy, what two approaches can be used to reach middlemen and consumers?
16. What does Professor DeHay state is the idea behind pushing strategy?
17. According to Professor McCarthy, why is a pulling strategy used? What is involved in it?

**View the television program: "Marketing Promotional Strategy."**

## After Viewing

— Review and answer the Television Focus Questions. If you are uncertain of the information, or missed a point, view or listen to the program again.

— Review the Key Terms from your text and be sure you understand the Learning Objectives for this lesson.

— Take the Self-Test to check your understanding of the concepts presented in this lesson. Compare your answers to the Answer Key located at the end of the lesson. If you answered incorrectly, the key provides a reference point so you can review the material.

— Extend your learning by completing the Business in Action and Your Business Portfolio sections of the lesson.

# Self-Test

## True/False

**T   F   1.** Promotional strategy is the communication ingredient in the marketing mix.

**T   F   2.** A buying reason based on the characteristics of a specific retail outlet or brand of product is known as a rational motive.

**T   F   3.** The communication process is the channel that promotional messages travel to reach the purchaser.

**T   F   4.** According to Professor Jerome McCarthy of Michigan State University, the objectives of promotion are to inform, persuade, and remind.

**T   F   5.** Prospecting is a step in the selling process that identifies potential customers for a product.

**T   F   6.** When deciding what advertising media to use marketers must consider such factors as cost, lead time, target audience behavior, and the company's overall promotional budget.

**T   F   7.** Publicity has less credibility than advertisements.

## Multiple Choice

1. Which of the following is an element of the promotional mix?
   a. advertising
   b. personal selling
   c. publicity
   d. all of the above

2. Which of the following is an industrial buying motive?
   a. quantity
   b. quality
   c. rational
   d. location

3. An element of the communication process that involves translating an idea into a message is
   a. sending.
   b. encoding.
   c. decoding.
   d. feedback.

4. Personal selling provides the company with an opportunity to
   a. give customers individual attention
   b. focus on a specific target market
   c. adapt a message to the customer
   d. all of the above

5. According to Professor McCarthy of Michigan State University, a factor that influences the promotional mix includes
   a. number of states to promote in.
   b. stage of the product life cycle.
   c. personal preference of the manager.
   d. all of the above.

6. Which of the following is a type of advertising?
   a. local
   b. regional
   c. product
   d. national

7. Which of the following is a sales promotion device directed at middlemen?
   a. coupons
   b. trade shows
   c. samples
   d. premiums

## Business in Action

This exercise is designed to have you investigate the elements of the promotional mix.

**Step 1.** Identify a men's or women's clothing store and a grocery store.

**Step 2.** Interview the managers of each store and ask the following questions:

 — When you develop your promotional plan for your store, what role do advertising, personal selling, sales promotion, and publicity play?
 — What percentage of your promotional plan is assigned to each element (i.e., how important is personal selling—50 percent)?
 — Why did you assign that percentage to each element?

**Step 3.** Record the answers to these questions.

**Step 4.** Compare the results of your two interviews and answer the following questions:

— What unique elements of the products sold required that the elements have different importance in each store?

— Which store relied more heavily on personal selling? Why?

— Which store relied more heavily on sales promotion devices? Why?

— What conclusions can you draw about the composition of the promotional mix?

**Step 5.** Summarize your answers.

# Your Business Portfolio

This exercise is designed to involve you in analyzing a company's promotional mix by monitoring a company's promotional program for a product.

**Step 1.** Select a national brand consumer product from the following: breakfast cereal, soup, T.V. dinner, frozen orange juice.

**Step 2.** Analyze the company's promotional program for this product by:

— Identifying the target market for which the product has been created.

— Identifying the company's use of the elements of the promotional mix.

— Advertising
   a. Locate examples of the company's advertising in newspapers and magazines as well as on radio and television.
   b. For each advertisement identify the central message.
   c. Compare the themes of the advertisements for specific purposes.

— Personal Selling
   a. Contact the stores the product is sold in and speak to the appropriate managers.
   b. Determine what role the product's representative had in negotiating shelf space as well as the support provided by the company for sales promotional efforts.

— Sales Promotion
   a. During your discussion with the store representative, determine the sales promotion efforts directed at the store.
   b. Determine the sales promotion efforts directed at the consumer by (1) going to the store and observing promotional signs, examining

the product for coupons, bonuses, and enclosures, and (2) monitoring direct mail and advertising for sales promotion ideas.

c. Analyze the purpose of each sales promotion idea.

— Publicity

Monitor the media to identify any free advertising provided the company or its product. (Specifically note any events that are sponsored or supported by the company and the product.)

**Step 3.** Summarize your findings in each area.

**Step 4.** Analyze your findings to:

— Determine the role each element of promotion plays in promoting the product.
— Determine the purpose of using more than one type of advertising and sales promotion (if they were used).
— Determine the degree of importance and emphasis placed on each element in the promotional mix.

## Answer Key

The Answer Key provides a reference for each question: T (text page), TG (Telecourse Guide page), or V (video program).

True/False

1. **T** (T 306, TG 98, V)
2. **F** (T 303)
3. **T** (T 306, 307)
4. **T** (V)
5. **T** (T 308)
6. **T** (T 311)
7. **F** (T 316)

Multiple Choice

1. **d** (T 306, TG 98, V)
2. **b** (T 304, TG 98)
3. **b** (T 307)
4. **d** (T 308)
5. **b** (V)
6. **c** (T 311, TG 98, V)
7. **b** (T 318)

# Lesson

# 14

# Marketing Distribution Strategy

## Learning Objectives

After studying this lesson, you should be able to:

1. Describe the importance of distribution in marketing strategy.
2. Describe the two components of distribution strategy.
3. Define marketing channels.
4. List and explain the primary distribution channels for consumer and industrial goods.
5. Identify factors that influence the channel selection decision.
6. Explain the reasons for using channel intermediaries.
7. Describe the types of wholesalers and their functions.
8. Describe the types of retailers and their functions.
9. Explain the components of a physical distribution system.
10. Describe the advantages and disadvantages of the five modes of transportation utilized in distribution.

## Overview

Did you ever want a pint of ice cream when the store was closed? Have you ever needed to replace a part in a lawn mower, vacuum cleaner, typewriter, or automobile and found that the store did not have the part, but would be getting a shipment in 10 days? If any of these experiences are familiar, you have had firsthand experience with the importance of distribution strategy—one of the four elements of the marketing mix introduced in Lesson 11, Marketing Concepts. The role of distribution strategy is to get the product to the right place at the right time. For products to have any value, people must have the goods where and when they want them.

Distribution involves two elements: the routes goods take from producer to consumer (channels of distribution) and the activities actually entailed in getting the goods to the consumer (a physical distribution system). Each element is critical in making sure the goods arrive when and where they are needed by the consumer.

All products do not travel by the same channel to reach the consumer. There are two major distribution channel categories: channels for industrial goods and channels for consumer goods. Within each of these categories are a number of variations.

Each of these channel categories, and the variations within, rely heavily on channel intermediaries, or middlemen. Intermediaries perform the various marketing functions of buying, selling, storing, transporting, risk taking, financing, obtaining market information, and standardizing and grading. The manufacturer's use of intermediaries in the channel depends on a number of factors, including the degree of market coverage desired by the manufacturer (intensive, selective, or exclusive), the type of product, the particular market segment, the action of competitors, the ability of the manufacturer to perform the marketing functions, and the geographic locations of the market segment.

Two types of middlemen operate between the manufacturer and the consumer: wholesalers and retailers. Wholesalers are middlemen who sell goods to retailers, other wholesalers, and industrial users, but do not sell in significant amounts to the final consumer. All wholesalers are not the same. Some take title to the goods, while others do not. Some provide a full range of services, while others simply resell goods and provide few services. With this variety of wholesalers, manufacturers can select one based on their needs.

Retailers, the second category of middlemen, are the last stage in the channel of distribution. They perform the business activities involved in the sale of goods and services to the ultimate consumer for personal use. Retailing activities involve in-store retailers and out-of-store retailers (house-to-house, vending machines, telephones, mail-order firms). In turn, in-store retailers can be classified by the number of outlets (independent or chain) and by the type of store (convenience, supermarket, superstore, specialty, department, discount, hypermarket, or factory outlet).

The second element of distribution strategy involves the creation of a physical distribution system. The system is the activities that take place as the goods move through the channels. These activities include warehousing, order processing, materials handling, transportation, and inventory control. Within this system another element is the actual transportation modes or means of shipping the goods. There are five modes (railroads, trucks, waterways, pipelines, and airways), each of which has its own strengths and limitations.

## Before Viewing

— Review the Overview and Learning Objectives for this lesson.
— Read the following assignment from the text *before* watching the television segment:

Straub and Attner, *Introduction to Business*, Third Edition, Chapter 12, pages 328–342.

— Define the Key Terms listed in the next section.

— Review the Television Focus Questions and take notes on the questions when viewing each program.

## Key Terms

Terms are referenced to a page of the text.

**chain store** (p. 337)

**channel of distribution** (p. 331)

**convenience store** (p. 337)

**department store** (p. 338)

**discount store** (p. 338)

**exclusive distribution** (p. 332)

**factory outlet** (p. 339)

**house-to-house retailing** (p. 340)

**hypermarket** (p. 339)

**independent store** (p. 336)

**intensive distribution** (p. 332)

**inventory control** (p. 341)

**mail-order retailing** (p. 340)

**materials handling** (p. 341)

**order processing** (p. 341)

**physical distribution system** (p. 341)

**retailers** (p. 335)

**selective distribution** (p. 332)

**specialty store** (p. 338)

**supermarket** (p. 337)

**superstore** (p. 337)

**telephone retailing** (p. 340)

**transportation** (p. 341)

**vending-machine retailing** (p. 340)

**warehousing** (p. 341)

**wholesalers** (p. 334)

## Television Focus Questions

1. What is the role and importance of distribution strategy according to Professor John Coyle of Penn State University?

2. What are the two elements of distribution strategy noted by Professor Donald Bowersox of Michigan State University?

3. What are the two basic distribution channels described by Professor John Coyle? Which channel requires a more elaborate distribution channel?

4. What reason is given by Professor Donald Bowersox for using channel intermediaries like retailers and wholesalers?

5. How does Professor John Coyle distinguish between wholesalers and retailers? What has happened in the marketplace to blur this distinction?

6. What four factors cited by Professor Bowersox should be considered in designing a distribution channel? What three styles of distribution are potential options?

7. What considerations are noted by Professor Coyle in deciding to use long or short channels?

8. What activities does Professor Bowersox include in the process of moving the goods through the channels?

9. How does Professor Coyle describe each of the activities or logistics included in moving the goods through the channels?

10. According to Mo Siegel, president of Celestial Seasonings, what was the initial distribution problem he faced? How was the problem solved?

11. What three distinct distribution channels for Celestial Seasonings' products are cited by Mo Siegel?

12. What advantages and disadvantages of using grocery distributors are noted by Mo Siegel?

13. What pros and cons of going directly into the chain supermarket does Mo Siegel describe?

14. How does Mo Siegel say the channels compare against each other?

15. How does Mo Siegel describe the importance of middlemen in Celestial Seasonings' distribution network? What do they do specifically?

**View the television program "Marketing Distribution Strategy."**

## After Viewing

- Review and answer the Television Focus Questions. If you are uncertain of the information, or missed a point, view or listen to the program again.
- Review the Key Terms from your text and be sure you understand the Learning Objectives for this lesson.
- Take the Self-Test to check your understanding of the concepts presented in this lesson. Compare your answers to the Answer Key located at the end of the lesson. If you answered incorrectly, the key provides a reference point so you can review the material.
- Extend your learning by completing the Business in Action and Your Business Portfolio sections of the lesson.

## Self-Test

True/False

T  F  1. Distribution strategy involves determining what the consumer will receive.

T  F  2. Distribution places the product where it is needed.

T  F  3. A channel of distribution is composed of trucks and railroads.

T   F   4. According to Professor Donald Bowersox of Michigan State University, distribution strategy involves logistics management only.

T   F   5. For industrial goods, direct distribution is used if goods are awkward to handle.

T   F   6. In-store retailers can be classified by the type of ownership and by the type of store.

T   F   7. According to Mo Siegel, president of Celestial Seasonings, the initial distribution channel for the company was direct to chain supermarkets.

## Multiple Choice

1. Which of the following is an element of distribution strategy?
   a. accounting
   b. financing
   c. research
   d. materials handling

2. Which of the following is a major channel of distribution category?
   a. institutional goods channel
   b. industrial goods channel
   c. individual goods channel
   d. discretionary goods channel

3. According to Professor Donald Bowersox of Michigan State University, a factor to be considered in selecting a distribution channel includes
   a. the resources available.
   b. the target market.
   c. the quality of the product.
   d. the degree of control needed.

4. Which of the following is a type of market coverage that influences channel selection?
   a. controlled
   b. intuitive
   c. intensive
   d. external

5. Which of the following is a food-based store that carries a variety of other products?
   a. chain store
   b. supermarket
   c. superstore
   d. specialty store

6. According to Professor John Coyle of Penn State University, a long channel of distribution
   a. is easier to exercise control over.

    **b.** is better utilized in large concentrations of people.

    **c.** is more difficult to exercise control over.

    **d.** requires more transportation.

7. Which of the following is a mode of transportation?
   **a.** railroad
   **b.** truck
   **c.** waterway
   **d.** all of the above

## Business in Action

This exercise is designed to have you investigate the activities involved in a physical distribution system.

**Step 1.** Identify a manufacturer or wholesaler in your area.

**Step 2.** Interview the person or persons responsible for coordinating the activities involved in physical distribution (order processing, warehousing, materials handling, transportation, and inventory control). In the interview ask:

— In your physical distribution system, what activities occur in the order processing area?
   **a.** What is the purpose of order processing?
   **b.** How are incoming orders received and by whom?
   **c.** What paperwork is originated in your area, and what is its purpose?
   **d.** Where is the paperwork forwarded?

— In your physical distribution system, what activities occur in the warehousing area?
   **a.** What is the purpose of warehousing?
   **b.** Are the products warehoused in specific areas? Why?
   **c.** What is the average length of time the products are warehoused before being sent to the retailer or wholesaler?
   **d.** Do you use public warehouses in addition to your warehousing facilities? If so, why? Where are they located?
   **e.** What paperwork is received in the warehouse relating to customer orders?
   **f.** What paperwork is prepared in the warehouse relating to customer orders?

— In your physical distribution system, what activities occur in materials handling?
   **a.** What is the purpose of materials handling?
   **b.** What activities are involved in materials handling?
   **c.** What equipment or systems (conveyor belts) are used in materials handling?

— In your physical distribution system, what activities occur in transportation?
  a. What is the purpose of the transportation area?
  b. What mode or modes of transportation are used?
  c. What factors influenced the decision to select the mode or modes?

— In your physical distribution system, what activities occur in inventory control?
  a. What is the purpose of inventory control?
  b. What activities are involved in this area?
  c. What paperwork is received by the inventory control area and from whom?
  d. What paperwork does the inventory control area originate? What is its purpose? For whom is it intended?

— How are all the activities in the physical distribution system linked?

**Step 3.** Record the responses to the questions and analyze the results.

**Step 4.** Diagram the physical distribution system on an 8½″ × 11″ piece of paper.

— Indicate the step-by-step process from the time an order is received until it is shipped.
— Trace the paperwork through the system.

**Step 5.** Discuss your observations of the physical distribution system.

## Your Business Portfolio

This exercise is designed to involve you in the development of physical distribution strategy.

**Step 1.** Select a product from the following: an upholstered living room chair, designer jeans for women and men, patio or backyard furniture, or a television set.

**Step 2.** Assume you are the manufacturer and evaluate your product by answering the following questions:

— How would you classify the product (convenience, shopping, or specialty good)?
— What type of market coverage is necessary for this type of good (intensive, selective, exclusive)? Why?
— What market segment do you intend to target?

**111**

— Where is this market segment located?
— What marketing activities are you, as a manufacturer, willing to perform?
— What marketing activities will you need intermediaries to perform?
— What channels of distribution are used by competitors?

**Step 3.** Record the answers to these questions.

**Step 4.** Develop at least *two* channels of distribution to your target market.

— Diagram the channels you selected.
— Explain why you selected these channels, using the answers to the questions in Step 2 as the basis for your discussion.

## Answer Key

The Answer Key provides a reference for each question: T (text page), TG (Telecourse Guide page), or V (video program).

### True/False

1. **F** (T 330, TG 105, 106, V)
2. **T** (330, TG 106)
3. **F** (T 331, TG 105, 106, V)
4. **F** (V)
5. **T** (T 332)
6. **T** (T 335, 337, TG 106)
7. **F** (V)

### Multiple Choice

1. **d** (T 331, TG 106, V)
2. **b** (T 332, TG 106, V)
3. **b** (V)
4. **c** (T 332, TG 106, V)
5. **c** (T 337)
6. **c** (V)
7. **d** (T 341, 342, TG 106)

# Lesson

## 15

# Marketing Pricing Strategy

## Learning Objectives

After studying this lesson, you should be able to:
1. Describe the importance of pricing in marketing strategy.
2. Identify and explain the potential pricing objectives of a business.
3. Describe how prices are determined by the supply and demand approach, the cost-oriented approaches of markup and break-even analysis, and the market approach.
4. Identify and explain ten potential pricing strategies marketers can adopt.
5. Explain the importance of nonprice competition through product differentiation in making pricing decisions.

## Overview

*That price is too high. I'll just wait until it comes down before I buy.*

*I don't see how they can sell it for that price. I'm just barely covering my costs.*

*I think we made the right decision. At this price we'll come in just under them and capture most of the market.*

These three comments describe the critical nature of the fourth element of the marketing mix—pricing strategy. It involves establishing prices for a product that will return a profit for the company. The ultimate price that is established must provide for the long-range profitability of the company. Equally important is establishing prices that will be seen by the consumer as a fair exchange value for the product. If the consumer is not willing to spend the money for the product, all the other elements of the marketing strategy have been wasted.

To be effective, the prices a company ultimately charges the consumer and its overall pricing strategy need to be made within a framework of pricing objectives. A firm can select from three general pricing objectives: sales volume objectives, profitability objectives, and other broad objectives (prestige, status quo, fair and ethical pricing).

Regardless of what objectives a company chooses, it must then determine the prices to be charged to the consumer. There are three distinct approaches to determining price: the supply and demand approach, the cost-oriented approach, and the market approach. The supply and demand approach considers the interaction in the marketplace, where the ultimate price is influenced by the actions of buyers and sellers. The cost-oriented approach, through the use of markup pricing or break-even analysis, focuses on the importance of organizations' building prices to cover their costs. The market approach recognizes that variables in the marketplace (political factors, the social and cultural environment, individual perceptions, timing, and competition) influence price.

By themselves, each approach brings an element of pricing into the spotlight: consumer demand, cost, or the actions in the market. But to effectively establish prices, all three approaches need to be utilized by the marketer.

Once a company has determined its price, it can adopt a number of potential pricing strategies. The choice of which strategy or strategies to implement will depend on the company objectives, the stage of the product life cycle the company finds itself in, and the actions of competitors. The ten potential pricing strategies are: skimming, penetration pricing, prestige pricing, follow-the-leader pricing, price lining, relative pricing, psychological or odd pricing, multiple-unit pricing, and leader pricing.

Each of these strategies places a company's products in head-to-head competition. Rather than engage in this type of strategy, some companies attempt to implement nonprice competition through product differentiation. In other words, if the consumers believe the product is different from competitive products, they, in essence, are not comparing prices.

## Before Viewing

— Review the Overview and Learning Objectives for this lesson.
— Read the following assignment from the text *before* watching the television segment:
Straub and Attner, *Introduction to Business*, Third Edition, Chapter 12, pages 341–352.
— Define the Key Terms listed in the next section.
— Review the Television Focus Questions and take notes on the questions when viewing the program.

## Key Terms

Terms are referenced to a page of the text.

**break-even analysis** (p. 345)
**break-even point** (p. 346)
**cost-oriented approach** (p. 345)
**demand** (p. 343)
**equilibrium price** (p. 344)
**fixed costs** (p. 345)
**follow-the-leader pricing** (p. 348)
**leader pricing** (p. 349)
**market approach** (p. 347)
**markup pricing** (p. 345)
**multiple-unit pricing** (p. 349)
**penetration pricing** (p. 348)
**prestige pricing** (p. 348)

**price** (p. 341)
**price discounts** (p. 350)
**price lining** (p. 349)
**product differentiation** (p. 350)
**psychological** *or* **odd pricing** (p. 349)
**relative pricing** (p. 349)
**skimming** (p. 347)
**supply** (p. 343)
**total costs** (p. 345)
**total revenue** (p. 346)
**variable costs** (p. 346)

## Television Focus Questions

1. What two points are made by Professor Jerry DeHay of Tarleton State University on the importance of pricing strategy?

2. What three basic elements does Professor DeHay identify that need to be taken into consideration in developing a pricing structure?

3. What three categories of pricing objectives are cited by Professor DeHay as potential alternatives for a company to select from?

4. What costs does Professor DeHay note must be considered in price development?

5. What does Professor DeHay say a company needs to do in evaluating the effect of supply and demand on pricing?

6. What reason is given by Professor DeHay for considering both cost and demand in developing a price?

7. What specific element of the marketplace does Professor DeHay note must be considered in pricing? What example is given to show the influence of market pricing?

8. Why is it necessary for companies to use all three approaches in developing their prices according to Professor DeHay?

9. What does Donald Zale, president of Zale Corporation, state is the pricing objective at Zale Corporation?

10. What does Zale state is the starting point in developing a price? What is added on after getting a picture of the costs?

11. What does Zale provide as an example of the influence of demand on pricing?

12. How does Zale Corporation receive competitive price information from the marketplace according to Donald Zale? Why is this information important?

13. What six price strategies does Donald Zale identify that are used in the marketplace by Zale Corporation? What is the objective of the loss leader strategy?

**View the television program "Marketing Pricing Strategy."**

## After Viewing

— Review and answer the Television Focus Questions. If you are uncertain of the information, or missed a point, view or listen to the program again.

— Review the Key Terms from your text and be sure you understand the Learning Objectives for this lesson.

— Take the Self-Test to check your understanding of the concepts presented in this lesson. Compare your answers to the Answer Key located at the end of the lesson. If you answered incorrectly, the key provides a reference point so you can review the material.

— Extend your learning by completing the Business in Action and Your Business Portfolio sections of the lesson.

## Self-Test

### True/False

T F 1. Price is the exchange value of a product expressed in monetary terms.

T F 2. The price paid by the consumer is primarily for the tangible features of the product.

T F 3. Supply refers to the quantity of a product that producers are willing to make available at a given price.

T F 4. According to Professor Jerry DeHay of Tarleton State University, if the pricing structure of a company is not right, the company simply will not make a profit and it will not survive.

T F 5. In markup pricing, companies use a combination of fixed costs, variable costs, and total revenue to determine price.

T F 6. A price discount is a deduction in the established price of the product.

T F 7. Making the product unique in the eyes of the consumer can only be accomplished through market pricing.

## Multiple Choice

1. Which of the following describes the importance of pricing?
   a. Pricing decisions can change with changes of managers.
   b. Pricing decisions are critical for the short-range survival of the company.
   c. Pricing decisions are critical to keep the product on the market.
   d. Pricing decisions are critical only from the consumer's standpoint.

2. Which of the following is a potential pricing objective for a company to select from?
   a. meeting competition objective
   b. sales volume objective
   c. being first in the marketplace objective
   d. underselling competition objective

3. Which of the following is a method for determining price?
   a. the sales volume approach
   b. the profitability approach
   c. the cost-oriented approach
   d. the status quo approach

4. According to Professor Jerry DeHay of Tarleton State University, when developing a pricing strategy a company must consider the
   a. political environment.
   b. costs involved in producing a product.
   c. convenience of the product.
   d. location of the business.

5. Which of the following is a pricing method that determines the number of units that must be sold at a given price to recover costs and make a profit?
   a. total cost method
   b. fixed cost method
   c. cost-oriented method
   d. break-even analysis method

6. Which of the following is a pricing strategy that sets the price high to relate the image of quality?
   a. image pricing strategy
   b. skimming pricing strategy
   c. prestige pricing strategy
   d. relative pricing strategy

7. Which of the following describes an attempt by a company to avoid head-to-head price competition?
   a. product modification
   b. product differentiation
   c. market segmentation
   d. product segmentation

## Business in Action

This exercise is designed to have you investigate both elements of pricing strategy: price determination and price implementation in the marketplace.

**Step 1.** Identify an organization that markets either industrial products or consumer products.

**Step 2.** Interview the person or persons responsible for price determination and price implementation for a product in the marketplace. In your interview ask the following questions:

- Price Determination for a Specific Product
    a. What are your pricing objectives for this product (volume, profit, other)?
    b. In building your price, what consideration is given to supply and demand, costs, and the actions of the marketplace (competition, timing, social and cultural factors)?
    c. How important is it from your standpoint to consider supply and demand, costs, and the actions of the marketplace in your pricing decisions?
    d. What method do you use in evaluating cost factors in pricing, break-even analysis, or markup? Why?

- Price Implementation in the Marketplace
    a. When you first introduce a product in the marketplace do you use skimming or penetration pricing? Why?
    b. In regard to competition in the marketplace, do you utilize either a follow-the-leader pricing strategy (reacting to others' prices) or a relative pricing strategy (setting prices above, below, or to meet competition)? Why?
    c. If you have more than one model of the product do you utilize price lining (distinct prices for the different models in a product line)? Why?
    d. Which of the following price strategies do you utilize once the product is on the market?
        1. Prestige pricing (setting the price high to relate the image of quality).
        2. Psychological or odd pricing (selecting price amounts that fall just below a major psychological threshold).
        3. Multiple-unit pricing (offering consumers a lower than unit price if a specified number of units are purchased).
        4. Leader pricing (selling attractive items at lower than normal prices).
        5. Price discount strategy (cash discounts, trade discounts, and quantity discounts).
    e. Why do you choose or not choose to utilize each of these strategies?

**Step 3.** Record your answers and analyze the results.

**Step 4.** Discuss your findings.


# Your Business Portfolio

This exercise is designed to involve you in the implementation of pricing strategy in the marketplace.

**Step 1.** You are to assume the role of a marketing researcher/price-conscious consumer for this exercise.

**Step 2.** Identify examples of the following price strategies by conducting a shopping tour of supermarkets, department stores, jewelry stores, or any other stores necessary to locate these pricing strategies.

- Prestige Pricing Strategy
  Product identified:
  Store name:
  Price:
  Why do you believe this is an example of prestige pricing strategy?




- Follow-the-Leader Pricing Strategy
  Product identified:
  Store name:
  Price:
  Why do you believe this is an example of follow-the-leader pricing strategy?




- Price Lining Strategy
  Product identified:
  Store name:
  Why do you believe this is an example of price lining strategy?

— Relative Pricing Strategy
   Product identified:
   Store name:
   Price:
   Why do you believe this is an example of relative pricing strategy?

— Psychological Pricing Strategy
   Product identified:
   Store name:
   Price:
   Why do you believe this is an example of psychological pricing strategy?

— Multiple-Unit Pricing Strategy
   Product identified:
   Store name:
   Price:
   Why do you believe this is an example of multiple-unit pricing strategy?

— Leader Pricing Strategy
   Product identified:
   Store name:
   Price:
   Why do you believe this is an example of leader pricing strategy?

— Price Discount Strategy
   Product identified, cash discount:
   Store name:
   Price:
   Why do you believe this is an example of price discount strategy?

— Skimming Price Strategy

Product identified, quantity discount:

Store name:

Price:

Why do you believe this is an example of skimming price strategy?


— Penetration Pricing Strategy

Product identified, trade discount:

Store name:

Price:

Why do you believe this is an example of penetration pricing strategy?


## Answer Key

The Answer Key provides a reference for each question: T (text page), TG (Telecourse Guide page), or V (video program).

### True/False

1. **T** (T 341)
2. **F** (T 341)
3. **T** (T 343)
4. **T** (V)
5. **F** (T 345)
6. **T** (T 350)
7. **F** (T 350, 351)

### Multiple Choice

1. **c** (T 341)
2. **b** (T 342, TG 114, V)
3. **c** (T 343, TG 114, V)
4. **b** (V)
5. **d** (T 345)
6. **c** (T 348, V)
7. **b** (T 350, TG 114)

# Lesson

# Managing Financial Resources: Short-Term Funds

## Learning Objectives

After studying this lesson, you should be able to:
1. Explain the role of financial management in a business.
2. Describe the business and economic conditions affecting the need for funds.
3. Explain the potential uses of funds.
4. Explain the basic sources of funds.
5. Describe the decision processes integrating sources and uses of funds in a business.
6. Explain the need for short-term funds.
7. Explain the sources of short-term funds.

## Overview

Just as the management of people, production, marketing, information, or risk is required in a business, so too is financial management required. A business cannot operate with any degree of security or consistency without purposely managing its financial resources. In most organizations this area is the responsibility of a chief financial officer. It is this person's job to develop and implement a plan for all the financial needs of the organization.

A business has a continuous need for funds. It is obvious that during a period of low company sales and revenue, or in an economic downturn, a company may need outside funds for payrolls, meeting suppliers' invoices, or taxes. Not so obvious is that during growth phases for the business and the economy in general, a business needs funds to expand its operations, buy more inventory, pay its suppliers while awaiting payment from customers, finance research and development projects, or invest in new markets or products. Additionally, businesses need money to bridge seasonal sales gaps and to provide support during labor strikes. All these factors affect a company's needs for funds.

Knowing that a business needs funds continuously, what are the major categories of needs for funding in general? A company needs funds to operate its business, to provide for the expansion and growth of the business, and to produce income. In the first area, business needs funds to meet its operating expenses. Although this normally should be provided from the sales of goods, there can be a delay between the actual sale and payment by the customer. To bridge this period, funds are needed to meet suppliers' bills, purchase inventory, meet payrolls, and pay utilities. Business also needs to have funds to expand its operations. This involves asset purchasing in the form of land, buildings, and major equipment. It also involves major investments in products and research.

Businesses meet these needs by utilizing short-term funds and long-term funds. Within each category there are numerous financing alternatives available to the financial officer. It is this person's responsibility to match the specific needs with the most realistic sources of funding. In doing this, the financial manager would use the following process for organizational funds management. He or she would:

— Determine the overall financial needs of the organization.
— Convert these overall needs into specific amounts of financing required for each project or category.
— Identify the potential sources of funds.
— Analyze each source to determine the amount available from each as well as the potential for utilizing it.
— Match the potential sources to the specific needs of the company.
— Acquire the funds.
— Establish a system to record the financial information, provide for feedback, and facilitate control.

Knowing the overall importance of financial management, the basic needs and sources for funds, and the decision process necessary to integrate the needs and sources allows you to focus on the management of short-term funds.

Short-term funds or capital is money spent on business operations covering a period of a year or less. Short-term capital is referred to as working capital. It is basically required to amplify purchasing power, pay current debts, meet unexpected expenses, provide a cash reserve if necessary, and allow the company to carry its accounts receivables while awaiting customers' payments.

**123**

There are numerous sources of short-term funds, including trade credit, commercial banks, factoring companies, sales finance companies, and commercial finance companies. In addition, commercial paper houses act as go-betweens in buying and selling company IOUs (commercial paper) to organizations with excess cash to lend. Another source of short-term funds is additional investment by the owners.

## Before Viewing

- Review the Overview and Learning Objectives for this lesson.
- Read the following assignment from the text *before* watching the television segment:
  Straub and Attner, *Introduction to Business,* Third Edition, Chapter 14, pages 388–399, 416, 417.
- Define the Key Terms listed in the next section.
- Review the Television Focus Questions and take notes on the questions when viewing the program.

## Key Terms

Terms are referenced to a page of the text.

**cash discount** (p. 396)
**cashier's check** (p. 396)
**certified check** (p. 396)
**commercial finance company** (p. 397)
**commercial paper** (p. 395)
**consumer finance company** (p. 399)
**draft** (p. 394)

**factoring company** (p. 398)
**line of credit** (p. 397)
**promissory note** (p. 393)
**revolving credit agreement** (p. 397)
**sales finance company** (p. 399)
**short-term *or* working capital** (p. 392)
**trade credit *or* open-book accounts** (p. 396)

## Television Focus Questions

1. Under what kind of conditions does business have a need for funds according to Professor Joseph Vinso of the University of Southern California? What examples are provided to support the answer?
2. What specific needs for capital are noted by Professor Vinso?
3. How does Professor Vinso describe the purposes of short-term and long-term funds?

4. What three elements does Professor Vinso include in the role of the financial manager?

5. What does Professor Vinso state is the importance of utilizing a decision-making model to acquire and manage funds?

6. What does Professor Vinso mean by, "Short-term funding allows us to take these hills and valleys and provide funds"?

7. What specific need for short-term funds is noted by Professor Vinso?

8. What sources of short-term funds are described by Professor Vinso? Which is the best source?

9. What four needs for short-term capital are cited by Paul Nichols, vice-president of finance for Quality Components?

10. How does Steve Miller, chief financial officer of Chrysler Corporation, differentiate between the short-term capital needs of the automobile factory and the Chrysler Financial Corporation?

11. What sources of funds are utilized by Paul Nichols?

12. How are the short-term needs of the automobile factory met according to Steve Miller?

13. What method, noted by Steve Miller, is utilized to solve Chrysler Financial Corporation's short-term needs?

14. What factors does Paul Nichols identify that influence the decision among the various sources?

15. What two factors does Steve Miller consider when selecting sources of short-term funds? What factor is important to the automobile factory? To the Chrysler Financial Corporation?

**View the television program "Managing Financial Resources: Short-Term Funds."**

# After Viewing

- Review and answer the Television Focus Questions. If you are uncertain of the information, or missed a point, view or listen to the program again.

- Review the Key Terms from your text and be sure you understand the Learning Objectives for this lesson.

- Take the Self-Test to check your understanding of the concepts presented in this lesson. Compare your answers to the Answer Key located at the end of the lesson. If you answered incorrectly, the key provides a reference point so you can review the material.

- Extend your learning by completing the Business in Action and Your Business Portfolio sections of the lesson.

## Self-Test

### True/False

T    F    1. Businesses only have needs for external funds during periods of economic downturn.

T    F    2. A factor that affects the need for funds for an organization is the seasonal nature of its sales.

T    F    3. According to Professor Joseph Vinso of the University of Southern California, during periods of expanding sales a company is going to have an expanding need for cash.

T    F    4. Generally, sources of funds for a business are categorized as short-term and long-term.

T    F    5. Firms use short-term capital or funds to purchase land, equipment, and other major assets.

T    F    6. A line of credit is a guarantee by a commercial bank that funds will be loaned when needed.

T    F    7. A consumer finance company provides short-term capital by purchasing the installment sales contracts that retailers have accepted from customers.

### Multiple Choice

1. Which of the following is a business or economic condition affecting the need for funds?
   a. filing bankruptcy
   b. period of economic growth
   c. meeting competition
   d. taking in new partners

2. The role of financial management is to
   a. develop a plan for travel.
   b. develop and implement a plan for all the financial needs of a business.
   c. assist in hiring personnel.
   d. prepare paychecks.

3. Which of the following is a step in the decision-making process for organizational funds management?
   a. determine the overall needs of the organization
   b. convert the overall needs to specific amounts for each project or category
   c. identify potential sources of funds
   d. all of the above

4. According to Paul Nichols, vice-president of finance of Quality Components Corporation, one of the factors that influences the decision on short-term funding is

    **a.** the company that is loaning the money.
    **b.** the time of the year.
    **c.** the effect on financial ratios.
    **d.** all of the above.

5. A source of short-term funds that involves the sale of open-book accounts is
    **a.** a commercial bank.
    **b.** a factoring company.
    **c.** a sales finance company.
    **d.** trade credit.

6. Which of the following is a commercial bank's binding promise that the money will be available to a borrowing firm if it requests it?
    **a.** promissory note
    **b.** line of credit
    **c.** revolving credit
    **d.** open-book account

7. Materials, supplies, and inventories are frequently purchased on
    **a.** factoring accounts.
    **b.** cash accounts.
    **c.** trade credit or open-book accounts.
    **d.** all of the above.

# Business in Action

This exercise is designed to have you investigate the needs for sources of short-term funds.

**Step 1.** Identify a retail business and a manufacturing business in your community. Interview the chief financial officer of each using the following questions:

— What specific needs do you have for short-term funds?
— Which needs are ongoing? Which are one-time-only needs?
— Are these needs anticipated, or are they emergency funding needs?
— What sources has the company identified to meet these needs?
— Why was each source selected?
— Does the organization have a financial plan to identify needs and acquire short-term funds to meet the needs?

**Step 2.** Record the answers to these questions.

**Step 3.** Summarize the results of your interviews and compare the needs and sources of each business.

**Step 4.** Discuss your findings.

## Your Business Portfolio

This exercise is designed to involve you in financial planning.

**Step 1.** Identify your specific financial needs for housing, education, vacations, household furniture, and automobiles.

**Step 2.** Identify specific sources of funds for those needs. These sources would include your income as well as short-term finance firms (banks, savings and loan associations, consumer credit companies, credit unions).

**Step 3.** Design a plan to match the specific needs for funds with the specific sources you would *consider* for each.

**Step 4.** Determine which sources you would utilize for each need.

**Step 5.** Explain why you chose each source to satisfy the need.

## Answer Key

The Answer Key provides a reference for each question: T (text page), TG (Telecourse Guide page), or V (video program).

### True/False

1. **F** (TG 122, V)
2. **T** (TG 123)
3. **T** (V)
4. **T** (T 392, TG 123, V)
5. **F** (T 392, TG 123, V)
6. **F** (T 397, 398)
7. **F** (T 399)

### Multiple Choice

1. **b** (TG 122, V)
2. **b** (TG 122)
3. **d** (TG 123, V)
4. **c** (V)
5. **b** (T 398)
6. **c** (T 397)
7. **c** (T 396)

# Lesson

# 17

# Managing Financial Resources: Long-Term Funds

## Learning Objectives

After studying this lesson, you should be able to:
1. Explain the importance of a firm's developing a long-range plan of growth.
2. Explain the uses of long-term funds.
3. Explain the sources of long-term funds.
4. Identify and explain the factors a business must consider in selecting long-term debt or equity financing.
5. Explain the effect of the use of long-term debt or equity financing.
6. Describe the process involved in issuing corporate stock to acquire long-term capital.
7. Distinguish between common stock and preferred stock.
8. Describe the process involved in acquiring long-term capital through bond sales.
9. Explain the type of bonds issued and the security provided to the buyer by each.

## Overview

In the previous lesson we introduced the critical nature of an organization's need for sound financial planning to provide a flow of funds to the company. Specific emphasis was placed on the necessity for, sources of, and uses for short-term funds. This lesson is devoted to the management of long-term funds.

As we discovered, short-term funds are needed to "grease the wheels" of the organization—to acquire inventory, to meet operating expenses, and to fill the gap until customers pay their bills. This is part of the funding environment. **129**

Another element of that environment is developing a long-range plan of growth for the organization with the capital to support that growth.

An organization cannot live hand to mouth. It must develop long-range plans for its existence. The company must address questions such as:

— Where do we want to be in the marketplace in 5 years?
— How geographically wide will our operation be?
— What additional products or services do we wish to add to our marketing package?
— What facilities and equipment locally, regionally, or nationally will be required to reach these goals?
— What human resources will be required to achieve these goals?
— What combinations of funding will be necessary to sustain our growth and reach these objectives?

The long-range plan will provide the guidelines to achieve the company's objectives. Long-term funds are needed to make major improvements that will enhance a company's ability to produce goods or services, improve product quality, invent new products, expand operations, purchase or remodel facilities, and purchase land and major equipment.

Huge amounts of money are required to build a new plant, purchase new equipment, or acquire land. To acquire the capital in the amount necessary, an organization has three potential sources: retained earnings, debt capital, or equity capital. With retained earnings the company is plowing back its own money. In utilizing debt capital the company is borrowing money that has to be repaid with interest either by long-term loans or by bonds. Finally, with equity capital the company acquires funds by selling shares of ownership through common or preferred stock. A company may choose to use only one of these sources or develop a package of two or more options.

In the process of making the decision on the funding package, the company's leadership must consider a number of factors. These include what is owed in each situation, the impact on ownership, tax considerations, and flexibility for the corporation.

Each funding option has an impact on the organization. If debt funding is used it must be repaid with interest—the interest is a tax deduction. It does not lessen management's control because debtholders are creditors, not owners; however, it may lessen management's flexibility if there are restrictions in the loan or bond agreements. Equity funding, on the other hand, acquires no obligation to be repaid. No debt is added to the company, but it does limit management's control by creating new owners. In addition, stockholders expect a return on their investment and desire dividends. Dividends are not deductible as expenses and are paid out of profits after taxes.

When a company chooses to utilize equity securities (common or preferred stock) or debt securities (bonds) it creates a prospectus and uses the services of an investment banking firm to successfully market the securities. The investment banking firm, or a syndicate of several firms, purchases the securities from the issuing company and resells them to the general public.

When a company issues common or preferred stock or sells bonds it does so with the knowledge that each type has its own advantages and disadvantages for both the company and the purchaser. Common stock has voting privileges, while preferred does not. Preferred stock has a prior claim on dividends as well as assets of the corporation if it is dissolved. In addition, preferred stock has a number of options that can make it more attractive to purchasers. Bonds have several options that can make them more attractive to the buyer and in turn impact management's control. The types of bonds include mortgage bonds, equipment trust bonds, income bonds, debenture bonds, callable bonds, convertible bonds, serial bonds, and zero coupon bonds.

## Before Viewing

— Review the Overview and Learning Objectives for this lesson.
— Read the following assignment from the text *before* watching the television segment:
  Straub and Attner, *Introduction to Business,* Third Edition,
  Chapter 14, pages 392, 399–417.
— Define the Key Terms listed in the next section.
— Review the Television Focus Questions and take notes on the questions when viewing the program.

## Key Terms

Terms are referenced to a page of the text.

| | |
|---|---|
| **bond indenture** (p. 408) | **long-term** *or* **fixed capital** (p. 392) |
| **bonds** (p. 400) | **odd lot** (p. 403) |
| **bond yield** (p. 410) | **preemptive right** (p. 404) |
| **capital appreciation** (p. 405) | **preferred stock** (p. 406) |
| **common stock** (p. 403) | **premium** (p. 408) |
| **common stock certificate** (p. 403) | **prospectus** (p. 400) |
| **coupon** *or* **bearer bond** (p. 409) | **registered bond** (p. 409) |
| **current yield** (p. 411) | **registrar** (p. 403) |
| **debt capital** (p. 408) | **retained earnings** (p. 400) |
| **discount** (p. 409) | **round lot** (p. 403) |
| **dividend** (p. 403) | **sinking fund** (p. 409) |
| **equity capital** (p. 400) | **stock dividend** (p. 404) |
| **fully registered bond** (p. 409) | **stock split** (p. 404) |
| **investment banking firm** (p. 402) | **transfer agent** (p. 403) |
| **leverage** *or* **trading on the equity** (p. 416) | **warrant** (p. 404) |
| | **yield to maturity** (p. 411) |

## Television Focus Questions

1. How is long-term funding defined by Professor Joseph Vinso of the University of Southern California?

2. Why is it important to plan for long-term funding according to Professor Joseph Vinso?

3. What does Professor Joseph Vinso include as key elements of long-term fund planning?

4. What specific activities does Professor Vinso specify that need to occur after funds have been obtained and projects are identified?

5. What are the two sources of long-term funding noted by Professor Vinso? How are each described?

6. What specific needs for funding does Paul Nichols, vice-president of finance for Quality Components, state challenged his company?

7. What sources did Paul Nichols acquire to solve these needs?

8. What was accomplished by this approach to funding according to Paul Nichols?

9. What specific factors does Paul Nichols cite that were considered before the decision?

10. What were the two areas Paul Nichols cites that were impacted by the choice of funding?

11. What was the specific long-term funding problem facing Chrysler Corporation according to Steve Miller, chief financial officer of Chrysler Corporation?

12. What actions does Steve Miller state were taken?

13. What does Steve Miller state are the results of the long-term funding?

14. As the loan was being repaid, what new funding need emerged according to Steve Miller?

15. What reason is given by Steve Miller for the choice of equity capital?

16. What process does Steve Miller cite was involved in the stock issue?

**View the television program "Managing Financial Resources: Long-Term Funds."**

## After Viewing

— Review and answer the Television Focus Questions. If you are uncertain of the information, or missed a point, view or listen to the program again.

— Review the Key Terms from your text and be sure you understand the Learning Objectives for this lesson.

— Take the Self-Test to check your understanding of the concepts presented in this lesson. Compare your answers to the Answer Key located at the end of the lesson. If you answered incorrectly, the key provides a reference point so you can review the material.

— Extend your learning by completing the Business in Action and Your Business Portfolio sections of the lesson.

## Self-Test

### True/False

T   F   **1.** An organization can operate with a series of short-range plans rather than developing a long-range growth plan.

T   F   **2.** A critical use for long-term funds is to provide for improving or expanding its existing lines of products.

T   F   **3.** When deciding on which source of funds to utilize, companies must consider the tax implications.

T   F   **4.** According to Professor Joseph Vinso of the University of Southern California, if long-term funding is not planned for, a company may not be able to get the amount needed when it is needed.

T   F   **5.** A prospectus includes information on the issuing company's financial status.

T   F   **6.** Preferred stock dividends are guaranteed by law.

T   F   **7.** A bond indenture is an agreement that states the bond's interest rate, maturity date, and other terms and conditions.

### Multiple Choice

**1.** Long-term funds are needed to
   **a.** "grease the wheels."
   **b.** purchase major equipment (fixed assets).
   **c.** purchase inventory.
   **d.** pay employees.

**2.** A source of long-term funds is
   **a.** trade credit.
   **b.** special savings.
   **c.** equity capital.
   **d.** 60-day notes with banks.

3. Which of the following is a factor a business must consider in selecting long-term or equity financing?
   a. the wishes of the stockholders
   b. the impact on management control
   c. the position of the company in the marketplace
   d. the type of product sold

4. According to Professor Joseph Vinso of the University of Southern California, equity funding
   a. eliminates the need for a prospectus.
   b. is a tax deduction.
   c. is considered ownership of the organization.
   d. is preferred to debt funding.

5. If a company chooses to utilize debt financing it
   a. lessens its control.
   b. creates a tax burden.
   c. incurs an obligation to repay.
   d. discourages its stockholders.

6. Common stock
   a. has voting rights.
   b. is guaranteed dividends.
   c. has priority rights to the assets of the company.
   d. is debt capital.

7. A bond that is unsecured and backed only by the company's reputation is
   a. a mortgage bond.
   b. an equipment trust bond.
   c. a debenture bond.
   d. all of the above.

## Business in Action

This exercise is designed to have you investigate the elements of long-term capital funding.

**Step 1.** Identify a company in your community that is in the process of expanding its operations (updating equipment, building new facilities or remodeling existing ones, increasing the number of locations, adding product lines).

**Step 2.** Interview the chief financial officer and ask the following questions:

— What forms of long-term funds did you consider in financing the major capital improvements?

— Which forms did you select? Why?

— What factors did you consider in making your choice?

— What is the long-term impact of the decision on the financial obligations of the company?

— What advice did you seek in making the decision?

— Who was involved in the decision?

— What role did a long-range growth plan for the company play in the decision?

**Step 3.** Record the answers to these questions.

**Step 4.** Summarize and discuss your findings.

## Your Business Portfolio

This exercise is designed to involve you in managing long-term funds.

**Step 1.** Develop a long-range plan for capital acquisition to finance the following: college tuition for children, an initial home or a larger home, major home improvements, major appliance purchases—refrigerator, washing machine, clothes dryer, freezer.

**Step 2.** Identify in your long-range plan the amount of capital necessary, potential source or sources of funds, a priority ranking of these potential uses of the funds, the amount of time needed to complete each part of your purchase plan, and the impact of these acquisitions on your operating revenue (income). Here is an example:

| Use | Funds | Source | Priority | Time | Impact |
|---|---|---|---|---|---|
| Initial home | $100,000 | 15-year fixed-rate mortgage | Number 2 | Within 5 years | 35% of present monthly income |

**Step 3.** Summarize your findings.

## Answer Key

The Answer Key provides a reference for each question: T (text page), TG (Telecourse Guide page), or V (video program).

### True/False

1. **F** (TG 130)
2. **T** (T 392)

### Multiple Choice

1. **b** (T 399, TG 130, V)
2. **c** (T 400, TG 130, V)

3.  **T** (TG 130, V)
4.  **T** (V)
5.  **T** (T 400)
6.  **F** (T 406)
7.  **T** (T 408)

3.  **b** (TG 130, V)
4.  **c** (V)
5.  **c** (TG 130, V)
6.  **a** (T 403, TG 131)
7.  **c** (T 413)

# Lesson

# Managing Risk

## Learning Objectives

After studying this lesson, you should be able to:

1. Explain the concept of risk and its relation to business loss.
2. Distinguish between the two types of risk.
3. Describe the role of the risk manager in company operations.
4. Explain the four potential strategies for dealing with risk.
5. Explain the importance of the law of large numbers, insurable interest, and insurable risk in the strategy of shifting risk to insurance companies.
6. Describe the various kinds of insurance a business needs and explain the role of each one in protecting against pure risk: fire insurance, business interruption insurance, motor vehicle insurance, workers' compensation insurance, public liability insurance, product liability insurance, fidelity bond, surety bond, life insurance, health insurance, disability income insurance, transportation insurance, power plant insurance, credit insurance, and hazardous waste insurance.

## Overview

In the daily operations of a business, managers and owners must contend with the possibility of risk. Risk is the chance of loss. The chance of loss is present in almost every phase of business activity. But what businesspersons must really guard against is the chance of severe loss—loss that can destroy profits and, ultimately, the entire business operation. One of the functions of a business is risk management. Like production, marketing, accounting, and finance, if the risk function is not managed well it can minimize the effectiveness of the business.

There are two kinds of risk inherent in business operations: speculative risk and pure risk. Speculative risk is a situation that may cause loss or gain—buying the right merchandise, choosing the proper location. On the other hand, pure risk is a situation that can only become a loss—theft of merchandise, customers harmed by a product the company makes.

How are these risks managed? Speculative risk falls into the domain of all managers. Following good business practices, researching merchandise, doing consumer studies, and analyzing accounting records are examples of ways to gain and not lose. Pure risk is the domain of a risk manager. A risk manager is hired by a business to identify significant pure risks that a company faces and prescribe techniques to deal with them. Risk managers are responsible for identifying the problem areas, analyzing both probability and the degree of severity of loss, and recommending appropriate strategies to deal with these problems. Risk managers work in three areas of risk: property, liability, and personnel.

Once a potential risk area is identified, the risk manager has four strategies to choose from: avoidance, reduction, assumption, or transfer. Avoidance is implemented when, after the company analyzes the risks associated with a venture, it chooses not to undertake it. Reduction is lessening the possibility the risk may occur as well as its degree of severity (for example, using fireproof building materials or installing a sprinkler system). When a company chooses to assume the loss it accepts the chance the loss will occur and plans for it (self-insurance fund to pay for any damages caused by the loss). A company may choose to transfer the potential risk to another organization (leasing equipment, insurance policies).

The decision on which strategy to use is based on the ability of the company to determine the probability of the risk occurring and to what extent this risk will affect the company. The less predictable the event and the higher the degree of severity, the more the risk manager should attempt to transfer it. Three factors used by a company to decide to transfer risk, and in turn by insurance companies in accepting the risk, are the concepts of the law of large numbers, insurable interest, and insurable risks. The law of large numbers is a mathematical calculation that determines the predictability of the loss occurring. An insurable interest is the idea that the person considering transferring the risk (or the policyholder from the insurance company's standpoint) must stand to suffer a financial loss before he or she will be allowed to purchase insurance on a given risk. Finally, to transfer the risk it must be categorized as an insurable risk. To do so, it must meet the five criteria of an insurable risk.

When a company determines that transferring a pure risk through insurance is to its advantage, many types of coverage are available. The amount of coverage and type of coverage depend on the particular business, its resources, and its philosophy of risk management. Generally, insurance coverage chosen by a business will be in the three areas of risk: property, liability, and personnel. The specific types of insurance to be selected from include fire insurance, business interruption insurance, motor vehicle insurance, workers' compensation insurance, public liability insurance, product liability insurance, fidelity bond, surety bond, life insurance, health insurance, disability income insurance, transportation insurance, power plant insurance, credit insurance, and hazardous waste insurance.

# Before Viewing

— Review the Overview and Learning Objectives for this lesson.

— Read the following assignment from the text *before* watching the television segment:
Straub and Attner, *Introduction to Business*, Third Edition, Chapter 15, pages 420–454.

— Define the Key Terms listed in the next section.

— Review the Television Focus Questions and take notes on the questions when viewing the program.

# Key Terms

Terms are referenced to a page of the text.

actuary (p. 431)
adjustable life insurance (p. 446)
allied lines *or* extended coverage (p. 436)
all-risk physical damage *or* multiple line coverage (p. 436)
annuity (p. 446)
beneficiary (p. 445)
bodily injury liability (p. 439)
business interruption insurance (p. 437)
coinsurance clause (p. 436)
collision and upset (p. 439)
comprehensive physical damage (p. 440)
contingent business interruption insurance (p. 438)
credit insurance (p. 449)
credit life insurance (p. 446)
deductible (p. 429)
disability income insurance (p. 448)
double indemnity (p. 445)
endowment (p. 446)
fidelity bond (p. 443)
group life insurance (p. 446)
hazardous waste insurance (p. 449)
health insurance (p. 447)
inland transit insurance (p. 448)
insurable interest (p. 428)
insurance policy (p. 427)

law of large numbers *or* law of averages (p. 427)
limited-payment life insurance (p. 446)
loss prevention engineer (LPE) (p. 431)
medical payments (p. 440)
mutual insurance company (p. 429)
no-fault auto insurance (p. 439)
ocean marine insurance (p. 448)
power plant insurance (p. 448)
principle of indemnity (p. 429)
product liability insurance (p. 443)
property damage liability (p. 439)
public liability insurance (p. 442)
pure risk (p. 424)
risk manager (p. 424)
self-insurance fund (p. 426)
speculative risk (p. 423)
stock insurance company (p. 430)
straight life insurance (p. 446)
surety bond (p. 444)
surplus lines coverage (p. 450)
term insurance (p. 446)
transportation insurance (p. 448)
uninsured motorist protection (p. 440)
universal life insurance (p. 446)
whole life insurance (p. 446)
workers' compensation insurance (p. 441)

## Television Focus Questions

1. How does Professor Don Hardigree of the University of Georgia distinguish between pure risk and speculative risk?

2. What reason is given by Professor Don Hardigree for a business to be concerned about pure risk?

3. When a company establishes an ongoing program of risk evaluation, what steps or processes logically occur within it according to Professor Hardigree?

4. What are the four risk strategies discussed by Professor Hardigree? What examples are given of each?

5. What does Dan McCoy, vice-president of Intermedics and executive director of risk management, personnel, safety, security, and office services of Intermedics, state is the role of the professional risk manager?

6. What three areas does Dan McCoy note that a risk management program focuses on? What strategies are utilized in these areas?

7. How does a risk manager attempt to identify risks according to Dan McCoy?

8. What processes does Dan McCoy note are used by risk managers to identify risk?

9. What specific strategies does Dan Hilder, assistant treasurer and corporate risk manager for the Signal Companies, utilize in dealing with risk in the area of liability? What examples of each strategy are given?

10. What specific strategies does Judy Tornese, director of risk management for Transamerica Corporation, employ to deal with risk in the area of personnel? What examples are provided?

11. What specific strategies does Dan McCoy use in dealing with risk in the area of property? What examples are provided?

12. What basic kinds of insurance coverage for the average businessperson are recommended by Judy Tornese?

13. What are the three rules of risk management according to Professor Don Hardigree?

**View the television program: "Managing Risk."**

## After Viewing

- Review and answer the Television Focus Questions. If you are uncertain of the information, or missed a point, view or listen to the program again.

- Review the Key Terms from your text and be sure you understand the Learning Objectives for this lesson.

- Take the Self-Test to check your understanding of the concepts presented in this lesson. Compare your answers to the Answer Key located at the end

of the lesson. If you answered incorrectly, the key provides a reference point so you can review the material.

— Extend your learning by completing the Business in Action and Your Business Portfolio sections of the lesson.

# Self-Test

## True/False

**T   F   1.** Risk is the chance of gain.

**T   F   2.** Risk exists in almost every phase of business activity.

**T   F   3.** A risk strategy of not undertaking a venture is known as reduction.

**T   F   4.** According to Dan McCoy, vice-president of Intermedics, in identifying risks the risk manager hires external investigators to analyze the potential.

**T   F   5.** An insurable interest is the idea that the person transferring the risk, the policyholder, must stand to suffer a financial loss before he or she will be allowed to purchase insurance on a given risk.

**T   F   6.** A coinsurance clause is a stipulation in policies that a company must insure a minimum of a property's total value before the business will be fully reimbursed for a partial loss.

**T   F   7.** Workers' compensation insurance is designed to reimburse employers for the loss of a worker's time when the worker is injured.

## Multiple Choice

1. The death of a key business executive is an example of a
   a. favorable risk.
   b. conspicuous risk.
   c. pure risk.
   d. speculative risk.
2. According to Professor Don Hardigree of the University of Georgia, a decision to utilize a deductible in an insurance program is a form of
   a. avoidance strategy.
   b. reduction strategy.
   c. assumption strategy.
   d. transfer strategy.

3. One problem with self-insurance is the
   a. difficulty of saving money.
   b. difficulty in predicting losses.
   c. possibility that the loss may occur before the fund is large enough to cover it.
   d. possibility that management may not cooperate with the decision to self-insure.

4. A mathematical law stating that if a large number of similar objects or persons are exposed to the same risk, a predictable number of losses will occur during a given period of time is known as
   a. an insurable interest.
   b. a quantified statistic.
   c. an insurable risk.
   d. the law of large numbers.

5. Which of the following is a criterion for an insurable risk?
   a. The risk must be expressed in percentages.
   b. The risk must be spread over a wide geographic area.
   c. A person must be self-insured.
   d. The premiums are unchangeable.

6. A type of insurance that covers a firm's losses when a key supplier's or customer's business is damaged is
   a. product liability insurance.
   b. compensation insurance.
   c. contingent business interruption insurance.
   d. safety-valve insurance.

7. Insurance that reimburses an employer for financial loss resulting from employee dishonesty is known as
   a. a surety bond.
   b. theft insurance.
   c. key man insurance.
   d. a fidelity bond.

## Business in Action

This exercise is designed to have you investigate the use of insurance by business as a strategy to transfer risk.

**Step 1.** Identify two businesses in your community, one a manufacturer and the other a retailer.

**Step 2.** Interview the owner or top-level manager in each and ask the following questions:

— How many employees do you have?
— Who do you transact business with?
— What types of insurance do you have on your business?
— What types of insurance do you have that are required by law, if any?
— For those areas not mandated by law, why did you choose to insure?
— Are there any areas you purposely chose not to insure? Why?
— What factors did you consider when determining the types of insurance to utilize and the amount to purchase?

**Step 3.** Record the answers to these questions.

**Step 4.** Using the information you obtained in Step 2, interview an insurance agent and ask the following questions:

— What type of insurance should a manufacturer of (whatever product your manufacturer interviewee produces) have? Why?
— What type of insurance should a retailer of (whatever product your retailer interviewee sells) have? Why?

**Step 5.** Record the answers to these questions.

**Step 6.** Compare the results of your interviews.

## Your Business Portfolio

This exercise is designed to involve you in managing pure risk.

**Step 1.** Identify specific instances in which you have chosen to apply each of the four strategies for managing risk by completing the following outline:

— Strategy of Avoidance
    **a.** I chose to avoid pure risk in the following situations:



    **b.** Reasons for use of avoidance rather than other strategies:

— Strategy of Reduction
    **a.** I attempted to reduce the probability of pure risk or lessen its severity in the following situations (burglar alarms, smoke alarms, etc.):

    **b.** Means of reducing the risk:

    **c.** Reasons for use of reduction rather than other strategies:

— Strategy of Assumption
    **a.** I chose to assume pure risk in the following situations:

    **b.** Means of assuming risk:

    **c.** Reasons for use of assumption rather than other strategies:

— Stategy of Transfer
    **a.** I chose to transfer pure risk in the following situations:

    **b.** Means of transferring risk:

**c.** Reasons for use of transfer rather than other strategies:

## Answer Key

The Answer Key provides a reference for each question: T (text page), TG (Telecourse Guide page), or V (video program).

### True/False

1. **F** (T 422, TG 137, V)
2. **T** (T 422, TG 137)
3. **F** (T 424, TG 138, V)
4. **F** (V)
5. **T** (T 428, TG 138)
6. **T** (T 436)
7. **F** (T 441)

### Multiple Choice

1. **c** (T 424)
2. **c** (V)
3. **c** (T 427)
4. **d** (T 427)
5. **b** (T 433)
6. **c** (T 438)
7. **d** (T 443)

# Lesson

# Managing Information

## Learning Objectives

After studying this lesson, you should be able to:

1. Explain the importance to a business of developing a management information system (MIS).
2. Explain the purposes of an MIS.
3. Describe the factors an organization needs to consider in developing an MIS.
4. Describe the types of information needed by managers for business operations.
5. Identify and explain the sources of information for business decisions.
6. Explain the methods available to acquire information for a business.
7. Explain the processes for analyzing data.
8. Identify and explain the tools available to assist business in communications and information management.

## Overview

Over the course of a day managers make hundreds of decisions on budgets, personnel, purchasing, products, expenses, and more. Because these daily decisions accumulate and become weekly and monthly totals, it is easy to see why management must have quality information to make good decisions. To have information "somewhere" in the company is of no use to a manager. Information must be accessible when it is needed and in a form appropriate to the manager's needs. The information must be managed. Therefore, the information management function in a business and the information manager responsible for creating a management information system (MIS) are critical to the success of an organization. This lesson is designed to explore the importance of the information management function in a business.

Regardless of size, *all* firms need to manage their information by constructing an MIS. This system is an organized approach to gathering data from inside and outside the company and processing it to produce current, accurate, and informative reports for all decision makers. A critical point to remember is that *every* firm needs an MIS. An MIS systematically gathers internal and external data, processes the data, groups related facts, analyzes those facts, and summarizes them into information for use in management decision making. Reports should contain information relevant to decision making to prevent the waste of a manager's valuable time and effort. In small firms like sole proprietorships and partnerships, the owner(s) may play this role. In large businesses the role is undertaken by an MIS department.

An MIS is not a haphazard collection of unrelated reports and data from the information flow. Its design is intentional to meet the needs of the organization. To have an effective MIS, management must identify sources of relevant data; feed data from these sources to a central clearinghouse; decide on the formatting and frequency of reports to be issued; convert raw data into such reports on a timely and accurate basis; and then get them to the appropriate users. The goal of an MIS is to provide what is needed (no more and no less) to those who need it (managers and other paid decision makers) at the right time and place and in the right form. The needs of the users are the key. The design of the system is dictated by the needs—the sources of information, the processing necessary, the type of presentation desired, and the report format.

To accomplish this, specific factors need to be considered by an organization in developing its MIS. These factors include:

1. Ensuring that the system is designed to meet the organizational objectives. The MIS must provide information to achieve the objectives of the company.

2. Providing information that flows logically through the organization structure. The information provided must be coordinated, usable, and logical for the user.

3. Delivering the right quality and quantity of information. The MIS must be responsive to the needs of the individual managers. This has two elements: different levels of management have different needs for information, and different functions (accounting, personnel, marketing) have unique needs for information. In addition, managers must receive the right quantity— not too much or too little. The MIS must facilitate their control of the decision making for an area.

4. Providing timely, accurate information. The information must be there when needed in a usable form.

Managers need all types of information for business operations:

— Top-level managers need information on competitors, economic conditions, legal and political developments, and technology to plan with. For

**147**

control purposes they need reports on the overall financial picture of the organization. This information can be supplied on a monthly or quarterly basis for trend analysis.

— Middle-level managers need information for their particular divisional operations. Whether the division is sales, production, personnel, or purchasing, the middle-level managers need information on trends or major types of fluctuations.

— Lower-level managers, because of the nature of their jobs, need daily information on performance. The needs vary by the position—a sales manager would want reports on daily sales, customer returns, new client contact; production would need reports on wastage, quality rejects, units produced, workhour variations; personnel might need reports on daily openings, interviews performed, and employees hired.

To gather this information for the unique needs of managers, a company must look to a number of sources. The data may originate from inside or outside the company. Internally, companies maintain records of sales, inventory, expenses, prices, and production rates. The firm may look externally for demographic trends, economic changes, and competitors' new products. Once the decision is made in terms of where the material data is to come from, a second element needs to be identified—Will it be primary data or secondary data? The data may have to be developed by the company itself because they are not recorded elsewhere (primary data). The alternative is to identify data that already exist; they are recorded somewhere (secondary data).

Once the sources of data have been identified, internal or external and primary or secondary, the company must actually gather it. If the data is already available (secondary data), either inside or outside the company, it is simply forwarded to the central processing area. If the data are not available, then they must be collected either by observation or surveys. The critical point to remember is that the needs of the users determine the data to be collected. It is a purposely designed system.

Once the data are collected they must be analyzed and summarized. To simply take total production figures for 6 months or total sales figures for 6 months and present them to management may not provide decision-making information. It may be more useful to show the average production for that period, or the average production for each worker, or to relate the production to the industry average. For sales, it may be more appropriate to relate sales on a monthly basis to the rate of inflation or the current interest rate. In other words, the data need to be summarized and analyzed to become useful. Three devices to aid in this process are averages (mean, median, mode), correlations, and index numbers.

Finally, for the information to be useful it must be presented to management in a useful form. A concise presentation of the information is needed— not mountains of reports. In addition to summaries, reports can be presented utilizing a pie chart, a horizontal bar chart, a vertical bar chart, a line graph, a statistical map, or a pictograph.

To facilitate the processing of these data into useful information, management has come to rely more and more heavily on the computer. Depending on the particular needs of the business there are various types of computers to consider including mainframe computers, minicomputers, and microcomputers.

A company does not necessarily have to own a computer to utilize it in its data area. A company may choose to use a service bureau, time share with other firms, or lease a computer. Regardless, computer application for management information needs are restricted only by management's imagination and willingness to change.

## Before Viewing

— Review the Overview and Learning Objectives for this lesson.
— Read the following assignment from the text *before* watching the television segment:
Straub and Attner, *Introduction to Business*, Third Edition, Chapter 16, pages 458–491.
— Define the Key Terms listed in the next section.
— Review the Television Focus Questions and take notes on the questions when viewing the program.

## Key Terms

Terms are referenced to a page of the text.

| | |
|---|---|
| **analog computer** (p. 474) | **memory unit** (p. 478) |
| **arithmetic mean** (p. 469) | **microprocessor** (p. 480) |
| **arithmetic unit** (p. 478) | **mode** (p. 469) |
| **array** (p. 469) | **output unit** (p. 479) |
| **computer** (p. 472) | **primary data** (p. 463) |
| **control unit** (p. 479) | **program** (p. 479) |
| **correlation** (p. 470) | **random sample** (p. 466) |
| **digital computer** (p. 477) | **sample** (p. 465) |
| **hardware** (p. 478) | **secondary data** (p. 463) |
| **index number** (p. 471) | **service bureau** (p. 487) |
| **input unit** (p. 478) | **software** (p. 479) |
| **management information system (MIS)** (p. 461) | **stratified random sample** (p. 466) |
| **median** (p. 469) | **time-sharing** (p. 487) |

# Television Focus Questions

1. What factors does Professor Omar El Sawy of the University of Southern California attribute to the need for business to manage information? What is the specific reason for managing information?

2. How does Professor Omar El Sawy define an MIS?

3. What does Professor El Sawy mean by "You want to make sure that you have the nuts and bolts before you have the bells and whistles"?

4. What factors does Professor El Sawy state must be considered in developing an MIS?

5. What questions does Professor El Sawy say need to be answered in designing an MIS? If a computer is used, what other considerations are there? After decisions about software and hardware are made, what else is necessary?

6. What is the most important source of information in designing a system according to Professor El Sawy? Why?

7. What overall informational need does Roger Leonard, director of management information systems for Sabine Corporation, state was being sought in the design of Sabine's MIS?

8. What differences are noted by Roger Leonard in the informational needs for the various levels of the organization?

9. What examples are provided by Roger Leonard to illustrate the distinct needs for information by different operating departments?

10. What three sources of data does Pat Wallington, director of information systems for the Exploration and Production Division of Sun Company, note are used in Sun's MIS?

11. What does Pat Wallington state is necessary to transform data into information?

12. What tools that are available to convert raw data into useful information are described by Pat Wallington?

**View the television program "Managing Information."**

# After Viewing

— Review and answer the Television Focus Questions. If you are uncertain of the information, or missed a point, view or listen to the program again.

— Review the Key Terms from your text and be sure you understand the Learning Objectives for this lesson.

— Take the Self-Test to check your understanding of the concepts presented in this lesson. Compare your answers to the Answer Key located at the end

of the lesson. If you answered incorrectly, the key provides a reference point so you can review the material.
— Extend your learning by completing the Business in Action and Your Business Portfolio sections of the lesson.

## Self-Test

### True/False

T    F    1. Timely, accurate, understandable data must reach decision makers at all levels if an organization and its people are to prosper and advance.

T    F    2. A management information system is defined as an organized approach for gathering data from inside the company.

T    F    3. Although in small business the owners usually function as their own informal MIS, all businesses need to have an MIS.

T    F    4. In collecting data a mail survey is ideal for reaching a dispersed group of people.

T    F    5. In summarizing and analyzing data, a mathematical method that provides a cause-effect relationship between two elements is the mode.

T    F    6. According to Pat Wallington, director of information systems for the Exploration and Production Division of Sun Company, computers have minimal application in the oil business.

T    F    7. To use a computer to manage information, it is necessary to own one.

### Multiple Choice

1. Which of the following does *not* describe the importance of a management information system?
   a. Information must be managed to be useful.
   b. It is adequate to have information somewhere in the company when it is needed.
   c. Information must be there in its proper form to be useful.
   d. Information must be there when it is needed to be useful.

2. Which of the following is a factor to be considered in designing an MIS?
   a. personnel requirements
   b. logistical concerns

**151**

      **c.** advertising constraints
      **d.** objectives of the organization

3. Top-level managers in a company need
    **a.** the same information as middle-level managers.
    **b.** information about accounting but not personnel.
    **c.** the same information as all other management levels.
    **d.** information on the overall financial picture of the organization.

4. Which of the following would *not* be considered internal data?
    **a.** sales results
    **b.** inventory levels
    **c.** laws affecting the business
    **d.** prices of goods

5. When primary data must be collected management has two techniques available. These are
    **a.** observation and computers.
    **b.** observation and government agencies.
    **c.** observation and surveys.
    **d.** surveys and library research.

6. According to Pat Wallington, director of information systems for the Exploration and Production Division of Sun Company, a source of data utilized by Sun is
    **a.** library research.
    **b.** data from someone else's data base.
    **c.** user surveys.
    **d.** government summaries.

7. Which of the following is a computer a company may consider using when processing its data?
    **a.** minimax computer
    **b.** mainstay computer
    **c.** microcomputer
    **d.** quantum computer

## Business in Action

This exercise is designed to have you investigate a management information system.

**Step 1.** Using your department at work, identify a summary report that is used in that department for management decision making.

**Step 2.** Identify the specific categories of information provided in that report. For example: employee hours worked, units produced, absentee status.

**Step 3.** For each category of information identified, determine the source of the information by answering the following questions:

— Did the data originate outside the company? If so, describe the source or sources.
— Did the data originate inside the company? If so, describe the department or departments responsible.
— Were the data primary or secondary or a combination?

**Step 4.** Identify how and by whom the data were analyzed and summarized to develop this information.

**Step 5.** Analyze the information on the report to determine:

— If the information is timely.
— If it is accurate.
— If it assists in meeting the objectives of the department.
— If it meets the needs of the individual manager or managers.

**Step 6.** Summarize your findings. Include recommendations regarding:

— Information that is included but not necessary.
— Information that should be contained in the report but is not.
— How to improve the format for presenting the information.
— The timing of the report.
— The people who may need to receive the report but do not.

# Your Business Portfolio

This exercise is designed to involve you in your personal management information system.

**Step 1.** Prepare an operating budget for your family unit for a 1-month period. (The budget is the management report document prepared by your MIS.)

**Step 2.** To prepare your operating budget identify the data that are needed as well as the sources of the data. You have two categories of data needed: revenue and potential expenses.

— Revenue
  a. From what sources do you receive data on potential revenue?
  b. Are the sources external or internal?
  c. Are the data primary or secondary?

— Expenses
  Use the following for expense categories: food, clothing, transportation, entertainment, medical, outstanding expenses (credit cards), travel, utilities..

a. From what sources do you receive data on potential expenses for each category?
b. Are the sources external or internal in each category?
c. Is the data primary or secondary in each category?

**Step 3.** In preparing your budget determine what factors you use to analyze the raw data.

— What items have priority? Why?
— Can any categories be increased or reduced based on the time of year? Why?

**Step 4.** Summarize your findings.

## Answer Key

The Answer Key provides a reference for each question: T (text page), TG (Telecourse Guide page), or V (video program).

### True/False

1. **T** (T 460, TG 147)
2. **F** (T 461, TG 147)
3. **T** (TG 147)
4. **T** (T 464)
5. **F** (T 469)
6. **F** (V)
7. **F** (T 487, TG 149)

### Multiple Choice

1. **b** (TG 146, 147)
2. **d** (TG 147)
3. **d** (TG 148)
4. **c** (T 462, TG 148)
5. **c** (T 464, TG 148)
6. **b** (V)
7. **c** (T 481, TG 149, V)

# Lesson

# Accounting for Profits

## Learning Objectives

After studying this lesson, you should be able to:

1. Identify and describe the functions of accounting that an accounting system is organized to perform.
2. Describe the six major groups that need accounting for decision making.
3. Distinguish between accounting and bookkeeping.
4. Explain the three elements of the accounting equation.
5. Explain the purpose of and elements contained on the balance sheet.
6. Explain the purpose of and elements contained on the income statement.
7. Describe the internal uses of accounting information by managers.

## Overview

In sports, whether it is football, basketball, soccer, tennis, golf, or swimming, there is a score keeping system to provide information on performance. There is the same need in business. Management can make informed decisions only if it has information on costs, expenses, profits, and performance. Management needs an ongoing scoreboard or health report on the business.

In a business this task of financial score keeping and providing information from that process is the task of the accounting function and the accounting system. A firm's accounting system is an organized approach to gathering, recording, analyzing, summarizing, and interpreting financial data to determine a firm's financial position. (A point to note: bookkeeping and accounting are not synonymous. Bookkeeping is a routine clerical function within the field of accounting. Accounting, as you can see, has a much broader scope.)

In addition to the management of a company, a number of different groups need accounting data for their decision making. Each group has a specific need that must be satisfied by the information supplied by the accounting system.

The groups include owners, potential investors, creditors, unions, and the government. Our major concern in this lesson is the internal need for and uses of accounting information by management.

Management and the other groups can be provided financial information by means of financial reports. Two of the most critical reports are the balance sheet and income statement. The balance sheet is an accounting statement that shows a firm's financial position on the last day of an accounting period or at a specific point in time. A balance sheet shows three major areas: assets (things of value the business owns), liabilities (debts or creditors' claims that a firm owes), and owners' equity (owners' claims against the company). The balance sheet illustrates the basic accounting equation:

Assets = liabilities + owners' equity

The income statement is an accounting statement that summarizes a company's financial performance for a period of time. It provides the manager with a tool to review the revenue and expenses of a business on an ongoing basis. Sometimes referred to as the profit and loss statement, it includes the revenue or income received by the business and the cost of doing business—cost of goods sold (if it is a business that sells merchandise), operating expenses of doing business, and profit or loss.

The information provided by the balance sheet, income statement, and other financial reports (like the statement of changes in financial position), serves as the basis for managerial decision making. The information in these statements, when analyzed further, provides the rationale for evaluating the performance of operating managers and the financial performance of the company and department; providing feedback on budgeting practices; identifying expenses that may need to be reduced; and identifying profitable and unprofitable products and product lines.

To provide this information the financial statements need to be analyzed further. This financial analysis can be done by comparing the performance of the company on a series of statements, and by comparing the performance of a company to other companies or an industry through ratio analysis of items on the income statement and balance sheet. A number of ratios can be used; the specific ratio to be used will depend on the information needs of management.

## Before Viewing

— Review the Overview and Learning Objectives for this lesson.
— Read the following assignment from the text *before* watching the television segment:
Straub and Attner, *Introduction to Business*, Third Edition,
Chapter 17, pages 496–519.

— Define the Key Terms listed in the next section.
— Review the Television Focus Questions and take notes on the questions when viewing the program.

## Key Terms

Terms are referenced to a page of the text.

**accountant** (p. 502)
**accounting system** (p. 500)
**acid test ratio** (p. 514)
**annual report** (p. 505)
**assets** (p. 508)
**balance sheet** (p. 508)
**bookkeeper** (p. 502)
**book value of common
   stock** (p. 515)
**cost of goods sold** (p. 506)
**current assets** (p. 508)
**current liabilities** (p. 510)
**current ratio** (p. 514)
**depreciation** (p. 508)
**financial analysis** (p. 511)
**fiscal year** (p. 505)
**gross profit on sales** (p. 506)
**income statement** (p. 506)
**inventory turnover** (p. 513)

**liabilities** (p. 510)
**long-term liabilities** (p. 510)
**net income** (p. 507)
**net income before taxes** (p. 507)
**operating expense** (p. 506)
**plant and equipment** (p. 508)
**rate of return on stockholders'
   equity** (p. 515)
**ratio** (p. 512)
**ratio of debt to stockholders'
   equity** (p. 514)
**ratio of net income to net sales**
   (p. 512)
**ratio of net sales to net income**
   (p. 513)
**revenue** (p. 506)
**statement of changes in financial
   position** (p. 511)
**stockholders' equity** (p. 510)

## Television Focus Questions

1. How does Professor Charles Horngren of Stanford University distinguish between accounting and bookkeeping?
2. What functions does Professor Horngren note are involved in accounting?
3. What groups does Professor Horngren identify that need accounting information?
4. What three categories of questions does Professor Horngren note that managers need accounting information to answer?
5. What are the two characteristics of information that distinguish the information managers need from what others need according to Professor Horngren?
6. What two sources does Professor Horngren identify from which managers can obtain the information they need?

**157**

7. What does Professor Horngren state is the value of the information contained on the balance sheet and income statement? What example does he provide to support this?

8. When does a balance sheet have value to management according to Steve Korby, chief financial officer for Tekton Industries? What important information is contained therein?

9. What does Steve Korby note is the value of the income statement?

10. What two ways does Steve Korby note that financial information is used?

11. What statement does Steve Korby make regarding information needs of managers?

12. What does Professor Charles Horngren identify as the two major responsibility areas of managers? Which financial statement is critical for each area?

13. What question does the statement of changes in financial position answer according to Professor Horngren?

14. What does Professor Horngren identify as a major tool managers use to give discipline to their planning?

15. What statement does Steve Korby make regarding the importance of a budgeting process? What is the value of the process?

**View the television program "Accounting for Profits."**

# After Viewing

— Review and answer the Television Focus Questions. If you are uncertain of the information, or missed a point, view or listen to the program again.

— Review the Key Terms from your text and be sure you understand the Learning Objectives for this lesson.

— Take the Self-Test to check your understanding of the concepts presented in this lesson. Compare your answers to the Answer Key located at the end of the lesson. If you answered incorrectly, the key provides a reference point so you can review the material.

— Extend your learning by completing the Business in Action and Your Business Portfolio sections of the lesson.

# Self-Test

## True/False

T   F   1. Accounting and bookkeeping have an identical meaning in business.

T   F   2. Owners need accounting data to evaluate their decision to become owners.

T    F    3. The income statement is also known as the profit and loss
              statement.

T    F    4. According to Steve Korby, chief financial officer for Tekton
              Industries, the income statement's primary value is that it
              provides you with a historical record of what you thought
              you could do.

T    F    5. Plant and equipment are categorized as current assets.

T    F    6. Information from the balance sheet and income statement
              need to be analyzed further to provide more useful
              information.

T    F    7. Information from the balance sheet and income statement
              are never related to each other by ratio analysis.

## Multiple Choice

1. Which of the following is one of the functions of accounting?
   a. gathering data
   b. relaying data
   c. returning data
   d. processing data

2. Which of the following groups needs accounting data?
   a. managers
   b. owners
   c. creditors
   d. all of the above

3. Which of the following is a category of accounts on the balance sheet?
   a. income
   b. revenue
   c. liabilities
   d. expenses

4. Which of the following is a category of information contained on the
   income statement?
   a. revenue
   b. assets
   c. liabilities
   d. equity

5. According to Steve Korby, chief financial officer for Tekton Industries,
   financial statements generally are used
   a. in firing managers.
   b. to provide information on a current basis to people who are managing
      the business.
   c. to change suppliers.
   d. in creating trusts.

6. The use of mathematics to bring important facts and relationships on accounting statements into sharp focus is known as
   a. creative financing.
   b. systems analysis.
   c. financial analysis.
   d. social management.

7. A ratio used to determine a firm's ability to pay its current debts from its current assets is the
   a. bank account ratio.
   b. cash ratio.
   c. current ratio.
   d. safety ratio.

## Business in Action

This exercise is designed to have you investigate the processes involved in using financial information.

**Step 1.** Identify a financial manager in a medium-sized or large company.

**Step 2.** Interview the manager and ask the following questions:

— How often is the company's income statement prepared?
   a. What value is the income statement itself to you?
   b. What specific items do you analyze on the income statement? Why?
   c. What ratios do you apply to the income statement information? Why?
   d. What additional information, if any, do you need to fully utilize the income statement?
   e. Where do you find this additional information?

— How often is the company's balance sheet prepared?
   a. What specific value is the balance sheet to you?
   b. What specific items do you analyze on the balance sheet? Why?
   c. What ratios do you use on the balance sheet? Why?
   d. What additional information do you need to fully utilize the balance sheet? Why?
   e. Where do you find this additional information?

— What other financial reports do you think are vital?
   a. What are their purposes?
   b. How often are they prepared?

**Step 3.** Record the answers to these questions.

**160** **Step 4.** Summarize your findings.

# Your Business Portfolio

This exercise is designed to involve you in the preparation and analysis of management information from financial reports.

**Step 1.** Prepare your personal income statement to reflect a month of revenue and expenses. In developing the statement utilize the following categories:

- Revenue
  Salary
  Interest, dividends
  Other

- Total Revenue

- Operating Expenses
  Rent
  Utilities
  Car expense
  Insurance premiums
  Groceries
  Entertainment
  Clothing expense
  Other

- Total Operating Expenses

- Net Income

**Step 2.** Prepare your personal balance sheet on the day you complete the income statement. In developing the statement utilize the following:

- Current Assets
  Cash
  Savings account
  Checking account
  Stock

- Fixed Assets
  Automobile
  Furniture
  Jewelry
  Home

- Total Assets

- Current Liabilities

- Long-Term Liabilities

— Total Liabilities

— Owners' Equity

— Total Liabilities and Owners' Equity

**Step 3.** Prepare both an income statement and a balance sheet at the end of the next month.

**Step 4.** Analyze the financial statements to determine changes, specifically, on the:

— Income Statement
   **a.** Was there any change in your total revenue? Why?
   **b.** Was there any change in your total operating expenses? Why?
   **c.** Was there any change in your net profit?
   **d.** If there was a change in the net income, what caused it?
   **e.** Does your financial analysis reveal any controllable expenses?

— Balance Sheet
   **a.** Was there any change in your total assets? Why?
   **b.** Was there any change in your total liabilities? Why?
   **c.** Was there any change in your equity? Why?

**Step 5.** Summarize your findings about the need for financial analysis.

## Answer Key

The Answer Key provides a reference for each question: T (text page), TG (Telecourse Guide page), or V (video program).

True/False

1. **F** (T 502, TG 155, V)
2. **T** (T 501)
3. **T** (T 506, TG 156)
4. **T** (V)
5. **F** (T 508)
6. **T** (T 511, TG 156)
7. **F** (T 515)

Multiple Choice

1. **a** (T 500, TG 155, V)
2. **d** (T 501, 502, TG 156)
3. **c** (T 510, TG 156, V)
4. **a** (T 506, TG 156, V)
5. **b** (V)
6. **c** (T 511)
7. **c** (T 514)

# Lesson

## 21

# The Environment: Business and Labor

## Learning Objectives

After studying this lesson, you should be able to:

1. Explain the basic principles of unionism.
2. Explain the primary objectives unions have for their members.
3. Trace the historical development of the labor movement.
4. Summarize the major legislation affecting labor-management relations and collective bargaining.
5. Identify and describe four reasons why people join unions.
6. Contrast the tools management and labor have to achieve their objectives.
7. Describe the roles of collective bargaining, mediation, arbitration, and a grievance procedure in labor-management interaction.
8. Identify and explain the current trends and directions of the labor movement.

## Overview

In performing the functions and activities necessary to operate a business, owners and managers do not operate in isolation. Their decisions and, ultimately, their actions and operations are influenced by a number of environments. These environments, including those created by organized labor, government regulations, economic conditions, social responsibility, and business law, affect what a business does and how it does it. Businesspeople need to be aware of these environments and include them as an element of their decision making. To ignore their presence or their importance will result in less than optimal operations. This is the first of five lessons focusing on the environments business functions in and is influenced by.

**163**

Whether a business has been unionized or not, it is influenced by the actions of organized labor. Businesspeople need to understand the purposes of labor unions, their objectives, and operating tools or strategies. Organized labor is one of the environments or factors that influence business operations.

What is a labor union? It is a legally sanctioned, formally organized association of workers who have united to represent their collective views for wages, hours, and working conditions. Unions are based on three basic principles: strength through unity, equal pay for the same job, and employment practices based on seniority. These basic guidelines serve as the cornerstone for all labor decisions and influence the objectives and tactics of labor.

These cornerstones were developed nearly 200 years ago with the early unions and have remained during the growth of unions. The labor movement has undergone a number of growth stages in its history. Originally considered unlawful conspiracies, unions evolved from craft unions to a position of power and influence. Accompanying the evolution of labor unions were various pieces of legislation, including the Norris-LaGuardia Act, the Wagner Act, the Taft-Hartley Act, and the Landrum-Griffin Act, that either facilitated or limited the operation of unions, depending on the general view taken by the lawmakers in Congress.

Throughout their history, labor unions have existed because they meet people's needs. People have joined and will continue to join unions—to acquire more power, to improve working conditions, to get or keep a job, and to improve economic position.

Labor unions meet the needs of their members and achieve their objectives by utilizing various techniques. These techniques or tools include strikes, picketing, boycotts, public relations, lobbying, and political activities. In turn, management employs various tools in its interaction with labor. Among these are plant closings, lockouts, injunctions, strikebreakers, management-run operations, employers' associations, lobbying, and publicity through the press. These techniques or tools may be used during the life of a union contract or during the actual collective bargaining process.

Collective bargaining is the process whereby employer and employee representatives jointly negotiate a contract that specifies wages, hours, and other conditions of employment. It establishes a process and a set of governing guidelines under which management and labor work through negotiation of contractual terms. In addition, collective bargaining includes the ongoing relationship between management and labor with administration of the contract.

What can management and labor do if the collective bargaining process bogs down? One approach is to implement the tools previously covered. Another is to consider either mediation or arbitration. Both of these devices attempt to resolve disputes and keep the parties working together.

Once a collective bargaining agreement is reached, both management and labor have agreed on a set of operating conditions and rights. Sometimes these conditions, rights, or interpretations of either one are the cause of disputes.

As a result, virtually all contracts include a grievance procedure, a series of steps to be followed by an employee whose complaint to a supervisor has not been resolved satisfactorily. In essence, it provides a safety valve as well as a remedy.

As we examine labor, another question arises. Where are labor unions heading? In recent years management has taken a harder line in dealing with unions. When this is coupled with the fact that the percentage of the total work force that belongs to unions has declined, unions have been forced to rethink their strategies and direction. Unions have focused their attention on new areas, including white-collar employees, high technology industries, and government workers.

Finally, business will always be impacted by labor and the labor environment. The future direction of that relationship hinges on the resources of each as well as their goals, individual expectations, and expectations of each other. Regardless, business must take into account labor in its decision making.

## Before Viewing

— Review the Overview and Learning Objectives for this lesson.
— Read the following assignment from the text *before* watching the television segment:
  Straub and Attner, *Introduction to Business,* Third Edition,
  Chapter 8, pages 204–234.
— Define the Key Terms listed in the next section.
— Review the Television Focus Questions and take notes on the questions when viewing the program.

## Key Terms

Terms are referenced to a page of the text.

**agency shop** (p. 219)
**arbitration** (p. 229)
**blacklist** (p. 220)
**boycott** (p. 225)
**closed shop** (p. 218)
**collective bargaining** (p. 228)
**craft *or* trade unions** (p. 209)
**employees' association** (p. 215)
**employers' association** (p. 222)
**Federal Anti-Injunction Act (Norris-LaGuardia Act) of 1932** (p. 212)

**grievance procedure** (p. 231)
**grievances** (p. 231)
**industrial unions** (p. 210)
**injunction** (p. 221)
**Labor-Management Relations Act (Taft-Hartley Act) of 1947** (p. 212)
**Labor-Management Reporting and Disclosure Act (Landrum-Griffin Act) of 1959** (p. 212)
**labor union** (p. 207)
**lobbying** (p. 223)

**165**

lockout  (p. 221)
mediation  (p. 229)
National Labor Relations Act
   (Wagner Act) of 1935  (p. 212)
open shop  (p. 219)
picketing  (p. 225)
primary boycott  (p. 225)
right-to-work laws  (p. 211)

secondary boycott  (p. 227)
simple-recognition shop  (p. 219)
strikebreakers  (p. 222)
strikes  (p. 211)
union shop  (p. 218)
union steward  (p. 231)
"yellow dog contract"  (p. 220)

## Television Focus Questions

1. How does Vicki Saporta, director of organizing for the International Brotherhood of Teamsters, describe a union?

2. What are the specific results noted by Vicki Saporta of having a union in the workplace?

3. Why do people join unions according to Vicki Saporta? What option is available to workers if there is no union to represent them?

4. How does Vicki Saporta describe the impact of a union contract on the workplace? What is the impact of the contract on the rights of workers?

5. What tools or strategies available to labor are noted by Vicki Saporta?

6. What does management need to do to have management-labor relations evolve in a positive direction according to Vicki Saporta? What has labor done to aid this evolution?

7. What does Vicki Saporta see as the key factor in better management-labor relations?

8. What reason is stated by Professor Quinn Mills of Harvard University for people voting to join a union?

9. How does Professor Mills describe the impact on the work environment of a business that is being unionized? Why is the environment much more formal?

10. What happens to the rights of workers and management with a union contract according to Professor Quinn Mills?

11. What tools are noted by Professor Mills that management has in dealing with labor?

12. What does Professor Mills see as the chances for labor and management evolving into a partnership with each other? What actions are necessary by both labor and management to achieve this relationship?

13. What two factors are cited by Professor Ben Burdetsky of George Washington University that affect the operating relationship of management and labor?

14. What point is made by Professor Burdetsky regarding the state of management-labor relationships?
15. What does Professor Burdetsky cite as necessary for relationships to develop?
16. In addition to cooperation, what other factors are necessary for the relationship to develop?

**View the television program "The Environment: Business and Labor."**

## After Viewing

— Review and answer the Television Focus Questions. If you are uncertain of the information, or missed a point, view or listen to the program again.
— Review the Key Terms from your text and be sure you understand the Learning Objectives for this lesson.
— Take the Self-Test to check your understanding of the concepts presented in this lesson. Compare your answers to the Answer Key located at the end of the lesson. If you answered incorrectly, the key provides a reference point so you can review the material.
— Extend your learning by completing the Business in Action and Your Business Portfolio sections of the lesson.

## Self-Test

### True/False

T   F   1. Management is not influenced in its decision making by the labor movement.

T   F   2. According to Vicki Saporta, director of organizing for the International Brotherhood of Teamsters, labor unions are a group of people who bargain collectively with their employer over wages, benefits, hours, and working conditions.

T   F   3. Right-to-work laws passed in states encourage the growth of unions.

T   F   4. The general trend in union development has seen union membership continue to increase as a percentage of the total work force.

**167**

T   F   **5.** According to Professor Quinn Mills of Harvard University, management has a responsibility to obey the union contract if labor-management relations are to improve.

T   F   **6.** A blacklist is a list of prounion workers created by management to deny the named workers employment.

T   F   **7.** Negotiating in "good faith" means that a party must agree to a concession asked by the other party.

## Multiple Choice

**1.** Which of the following is a basic principle of unionism?
   **a.** one person, one vote
   **b.** strength through unity
   **c.** power to the people
   **d.** control management

**2.** One of the objectives of unions is to
   **a.** preserve equality.
   **b.** ensure control.
   **c.** improve job security.
   **d.** motivate cooperation.

**3.** According to Vicki Saporta, director of organizing for the International Brotherhood of Teamsters, unions result in
   **a.** developing a positive work environment.
   **b.** creating a "them and us" climate.
   **c.** giving workers dignity and respect.
   **d.** motivating more productivity.

**4.** The Wagner Act (National Labor Relations Act)
   **a.** promoted the formation of unions.
   **b.** limited the formation of unions.
   **c.** provided for a minimum wage.
   **d.** was directed at both management and labor equally.

**5.** According to Professor Quinn Mills of Harvard University, a tool used by management in dealing with unions is
   **a.** implementing a boycott.
   **b.** creating a trust-busting unit.
   **c.** locking employees out.
   **d.** refusing to recognize the bargaining unit.

**6.** Which of the following is *not* a tool management uses to achieve its objectives?
   **a.** strikebreakers
   **b.** injunction
   **c.** lockout
   **d.** boycott

7. A process in which the third party has no authority to decide the issue in a labor disagreement is known as
   a. negotiation.
   b. arbitration.
   c. mediation.
   d. compulsory arbitration.

# Business in Action

This exercise is designed to have you investigate the labor environment.

**Step 1.** Identify a local labor representative. This person may be either the business agent or president of a local union or a union steward.

**Step 2.** Interview the person by asking the following questions:

- What are the goals of labor unions?
- What are the specific goals of your union?
- Why do you believe people join your union?
- What has your union accomplished for its members in this bargaining unit?
- How has the presence of your union affected the work setting and work environment?
- How do you believe you are perceived by management? Why?

**Step 3.** Interview a manager of a company that is unionized and ask the following questions:

- What do you believe are the goals of labor unions?
- What are the specific goals of the labor union in your company?
- Why do you believe people voted for a union?
- Why does the union remain in existence?
- What has the union accomplished for its members?
- Why was it necessary for the union to bargain for these accomplishments?
- How has the presence of the union affected the work setting and the work environment?
- How do you believe management is perceived by the union?

**Step 4.** Record your answers, analyze the results, and summarize your findings. **169**

## Your Business Portfolio

This exercise is designed to involve you in analyzing the need for and effect of a labor union in your work setting.

**Step 1.** Identify a company you have worked for or are presently working for that is not unionized.

**Step 2.** Rate your work environment by placing a number next to each statement using a scale of 1 (low) to 10 (high).

*Rating*

_____   1. Management listens to the suggestions of employees about policies, procedures, and rules.

_____   2. Management responds to the suggestions of employees about policies, procedures, and rules.

_____   3. I feel I can influence needed changes in the work environment.

_____   4. The working conditions are safe.

_____   5. The working conditions are constantly reviewed and improved by management.

_____   6. People feel secure in voicing opinions about the work environment.

_____   7. Promotions are made without favoritism.

_____   8. The salary I receive is comparable to the same job in other companies.

_____   9. Raises are determined without favoritism.

_____  10. Benefit packages are comparable to other companies in the area.

**Step 3.** Explain the reason for each rating.

**Step 4.** Add up your score and compare it with the following scale:

| | |
|---|---|
| 0– 50 | You are a prime candidate for a union. |
| 51– 65 | If you are moving up there's hope.<br>Watch out for the banana peel. |
| 66– 85 | Things are on the right track. |
| 86–100 | You have a good comfort zone. Enjoy it! |

## Answer Key

The Answer Key provides a reference for each question: T (text page), TG (Telecourse Guide page), or V (video program).

## True/False

1. **F** (TG 163, 164, V)
2. **T** (V)
3. **F** (T 211)
4. **F** (T 211, TG 165)
5. **T** (V)
6. **T** (T 220)
7. **F** (T 228)

## Multiple Choice

1. **b** (T 208, TG 164)
2. **c** (T 208)
3. **c** (V)
4. **a** (T 211)
5. **c** (V)
6. **d** (T 225, TG 164)
7. **c** (T 229)

# Lesson

## 22

# The Environment: Business and Government Regulation

## Learning Objectives

After studying this lesson, you should be able to:

1. Explain the interactive roles of business and government.
2. Identify the major regulatory agencies and their specific areas of involvement with business.
3. Describe the tangible and intangible costs of regulation.
4. Discuss the potential responses of business to regulation.
5. Explain the concept of deregulation.

## Overview

Business does not operate in a vacuum. An element in the environment that influences what a business does and how it does it is government regulation. As decisions are made about the company's products, pricing practices, advertising strategies, potential issues of common or preferred stock, and acquisitions of competitors, it is done with the consideration of government regulations and guidelines.

Business and government are not two separate worlds. The interaction of government agencies with business, either through required reports, compliance visits, or investigation of alleged violations, is a constant part of the business operating environment. The interaction takes place in virtually every area of a business's operations—production, employment, safety, competition. When various state regulations are combined with the federal regulations, business and government interaction takes on an even broader scope.

What government agencies regulate business? The principal federal regulatory agencies include the Interstate Commerce Commission, Federal Trade Commission, Food and Drug Administration, Federal Communications Commission, Equal Employment Opportunity Commission, Occupational Safety and Health Administration, Environmental Protection Agency, and Consumer Product Safety Commission. Their specific areas of involvement range from approving rates and routes for truck, bus, and rail carriers to investigating allegations of restraint of trade to setting standards for product safety. What is important for a businessperson is the *scope* and *complexity* of government regulation.

All the regulation that occurs in the business environment carries a cost, both tangible and intangible. The tangible costs are measured by the numerous hours of employees' and management's time to complete the required reports and to monitor compliance within the organization. The intangible costs cannot be measured but are evidenced in the general attitude of businesspeople—the general fear of making a mistake they may not be aware of, or the perception that the paperwork mountain will continue to increase.

What can businesspeople do in light of these regulations? Being frustrated and concerned is one response; but there are other alternatives to government regulations. These include improved self-policing; the use of lobbying; focusing on the results to be achieved, rather than the means of achieving them; developing a system of financial rewards and penalties; and moving toward deregulation.

Of these alternatives, deregulation has made the greatest initial impact. Basically deregulation is removing the governmental agency's controlling power over previously structured areas of business. A prime example is in shipping and transportation, where the deregulation of shipping rates and passenger fares has led to these being determined in the marketplace. The purpose of deregulation is to encourage the growth of productivity as marketplace incentives fill the gaps left by decreased government regulation.

# Before Viewing

- Review the Overview and Learning Objectives for this lesson.
- Read the following assignment from the text *before* watching the television segment:
  Straub and Attner, *Introduction to Business,* Third Edition,
  Chapter 6, pages 162–164, Chapter 14, page 401, and Chapter 20, pages 599–606.
- Define the Key Terms listed in the next section.
- Review the Television Focus Questions and take notes on the questions when viewing the program.

## Key Term

Term is referenced to a page of the text.
**Occupational Safety and Health**
  **Act** (p. 162)

## Television Focus Questions

1. What is the purpose of government regulation according to Professor Susan Tolchin of George Washington University?

2. According to Professor Tolchin, how does government regulation affect the overall business climate—both negatively and positively?

3. What specific intangible cost of government regulation is cited by Professor Tolchin?

4. What does James Troy, director of Region I Programs for the Equal Employment Opportunity Commission (EEOC), say is the purpose of the EEOC?

5. Why was the Occupational Safety and Health Administration created according to Barry White, director of safety standards?

6. What does James McCarty, associate director of the Bureau of Competition for the Federal Trade Commission, cite as the three purposes of the Federal Trade Commission?

7. What areas of the workplace does James Troy note are affected by the EEOC?

8. What does Barry White say is the major effect OSHA has had on business?

9. What two areas does James McCarty note the Federal Trade Commission has affected most?

10. What two specific areas of impact does James Troy say the EEOC has beyond its official purpose?

11. What changes does Barry White note have occurred in the way companies look at worker health and safety?

12. What example is provided by James McCarty to illustrate the Federal Trade Commission's impact beyond its charter?

13. According to Walt Humann, president of Hunt Oil Company, what are the tangible and intangible costs of regulation?

14. What alternatives to government regulation are presented by Walt Humann?

15. What does Professor Susan Tolchin identify as four alternatives to government regulation?

16. How does Professor Tolchin define deregulation? What has been the impact of deregulation?

17. Will deregulation increase or decrease according to Professor Tolchin?

**View the television program "The Environment: Business and Government Regulation."**

# After Viewing

- Review and answer the Television Focus Questions. If you are uncertain of the information, or missed a point, view or listen to the program again.
- Review the Key Terms from your text and be sure you understand the Learning Objectives for this lesson.
- Take the Self-Test to check your understanding of the concepts presented in this lesson. Compare your answers to the Answer Key located at the end of the lesson. If you answered incorrectly, the key provides a reference point so you can review the material.
- Extend your learning by completing the Business in Action and Your Business Portfolio sections of the lesson.

# Self-Test

## True/False

T   F   **1.** Government regulatory power over business is possessed only by the federal government.

T   F   **2.** According to Professor Susan Tolchin of George Washington University, government regulation has had only negative effects.

T   F   **3.** Business decisions must be made with a consideration of government regulation and guidelines.

T   F   **4.** The Interstate Commerce Commission regulates the interstate issuance of stocks and bonds.

T   F   **5.** The cost of compliance for preparing government reports is equal for large and small businesses.

T   F   **6.** A potential alternative to government regulation is to raise the prices of goods sold by firms that will not meet legislated goals.

T   F   **7.** Deregulation has resulted in price competition in both the airlines and transportation industries.

## Multiple Choice

**1.** Which of the following describes business and government interaction?
   **a.** They are two separate worlds.
   **b.** They interact in virtually all areas of business operations.

**175**

      c. It is confined to safety and employment.

      d. It is concerned with only large business.

2. Which of the following is a method of business and government agency interaction?

      a. court appearances

      b. television interviews

      c. compliance visits

      d. telephone reviews

3. Which of the following is a government regulatory agency?

      a. Food and Drug Administration

      b. Environmental Protection Agency

      c. Federal Communications Commission

      d. all of the above

4. According to Professor Susan Tolchin of George Washington University, the purpose of government regulation is to

      a. control business.

      b. protect business and the public.

      c. control commerce.

      d. protect commerce.

5. Which of the agencies sets standards of quality for food and drug products?

      a. Interstate Commerce Commission

      b. Consumer Product Safety Commission

      c. Product Quality Control Board

      d. Food and Drug Administration

6. An alternative to government regulation that focuses on consolidation of overlapping government authority and elimination of agency duplication of activities is

      a. self-policing.

      b. focusing on results.

      c. lobbying.

      d. penalties and rewards.

7. Which of the following is an industry that once was regulated but has been deregulated?

      a. grocery business

      b. transportation

      c. consumer affairs

      d. automotive industry

## Business in Action

This exercise is designed to acquaint you with the impact of government regulation on business.

**Step 1.** Identify a medium-sized or large business in your community and arrange to interview a top-level manager.

**Step 2.** During the interview ask the following questions:

— What government agencies regulate the operation of your business?
— What are the specific areas, processes, or practices that these agencies regulate?
— What benefits do the consumer and society receive from these regulatory practices?
— What specific actions or changes have you had to take to achieve these requirements?
— What have been the tangible costs of compliance to the business (employee hours, legal fees)?
— What are the intangible costs to the business?
— Are the tangible costs of the regulatory compliance absorbed by the company or passed on to the consumer?
— Do you believe government regulation is necessary? Why?
— What alternatives would you recommend to government regulation?

**Step 3.** Record your answers and discuss your findings.

## Your Business Portfolio

This exercise is designed to involve you with the scope of government regulation that falls directly on a business and indirectly on the consumer.

**Step 1.** Develop an activity and events log.

— This log is to be used to record the various activities and events that you experience that are affected by governmental regulation.
— The activities or events would include what you do during a day. For example: watch television, eat at a fast-food shop, drive your car to work, receive a paycheck, buy a carton of milk.
— For each separate activity listed, identify the governmental agency or agencies that regulate it.

Activity Event Log

| Activity | Governmental Agency |
| --- | --- |
| Watch television program | Federal Communications Commission |
| Interview for a job | Equal Employment Opportunity Commission |

| *Activity* | *Governmental Agency* |
|---|---|
| Buy tires for car | Consumer Product Safety Commission, Federal Trade Commission |

**Step 2.** Maintain this log for two days and record your observations.

**Step 3.** Summarize your findings.

## Answer Key

The Answer Key provides a reference for each question: T (text page), TG (Telecourse Guide page), or V (video program).

### True/False

1. **F** (T 599, TG 172)
2. **F** (V)
3. **T** (TG 172, V)
4. **F** (T 600)
5. **F** (T 601)
6. **F** (T 603, 604, TG 173)
7. **T** (T 605)

### Multiple Choice

1. **b** (TG 172)
2. **c** (TG 172)
3. **d** (T 600, TG 173)
4. **b** (V)
5. **d** (T 600)
6. **c** (T 603)
7. **b** (T 605, TG 173, V)

# Lesson

## 23

# The Environment: Business and the Law

## Learning Objectives

After studying this lesson, you should be able to:

1. Explain the meaning of law.
2. Explain the effect of law on business operations.
3. Identify the elements of the law that comprise business law.
4. Explain the purpose of the Uniform Commercial Code in business transactions.
5. Explain the law of contracts and its effect on business.
6. Explain the law of agency as it relates to business transactions.
7. Distinguish the law of sales from the law of contracts.
8. Explain the law of property as it relates to patents, trademarks, copyrights, and bailments.
9. Explain the law of negotiable instruments.
10. Explain the law of bankruptcy.
11. Explain the law of torts.

## Overview

Do you know your obligations when you sign a contract? Do you know how to protect your creative abilities with a patent? What exactly is the liability of an owner when a salesperson makes misleading claims? After reviewing these questions, one point is obvious—an element in the environment that impacts business and business operations is the law. A businessperson must make decisions with knowledge of the legal environment. Once again, business does not operate in a vacuum.

What exactly is law? It is a series of codes of personal conduct and regulations that collectively are identified as law. In terms of business, the two categories that influence personal conduct and regulate business are common law and statutory law. Common law is based on records of early English court decisions, while statutory law is a written body of rules created and approved by a group of persons generally referred to as the legislature.

How does law affect business operations? Law was created by a series of guidelines established either through previous court decisions or by designed legislation, which serve as boundaries of acceptable conduct in business operations. Because of the widespread nature of business operations, law affects the nature of every business transaction. When business creates contracts, sells goods and services, initiates checks to pay for the goods or services, hires an agent to represent the company, and provides the purchaser with a warranty on the product, both *what* it does in these areas and *how* it does it are prescribed by law.

The elements of law that are generally considered business law include the law of contracts, law of agency, law of sales, law of property, law of negotiable instruments, and the law of bankruptcy. In addition to these areas, business also is influenced by tort law and criminal law. A businessperson could be guilty of a tort if a customer tripped on extension cords lying on the floor in a store. Criminal law governs actions of embezzlement and fraud in business operations.

A dilemma facing a businessperson is how to function within the framework of the law when it is so complicated and all encompassing. If this same businessperson conducts business in several states, another variable is added—What do the states see as the correct form of negotiable instruments, contracts, and so on? Fortunately for businesspersons and business in general, this last problem has been minimized. The Uniform Commercial Code (UCC), a comprehensive body of business law that encompasses various kinds of business transactions, was drafted to ensure that business transactions will be handled consistently from state to state. It includes contracts, agency, sales, property, negotiable instruments, and bankruptcy. Let's examine each briefly.

— The Law of Contracts. A contract is a legally binding agreement between two or more parties obliging them to do or refrain from doing certain acts. When a businessperson signs a contract he or she becomes obligated to the other party. The businessperson gives up certain legal rights, and the contract becomes the governing body.

— The Law of Agency. In business it is often necessary to have other parties represent the business in sales or contract negotiations. The law of agency governs the actions of an agent who is authorized to transact business and exercise authority on behalf of another party.

— The Law of Sales. The law of sales governs business transactions that deal with the sale of tangible personal property for a price. Unlike contracts, sales agreements cannot be made on real estate, items that are negotiated rather than sold (insurance policies and promissory notes), or investment securities.

— The Law of Property. In its operations a business acquires and deals with property, both real and personal. Therefore, the businessperson needs to be familiar with the law of property. Of particular interest to businesspersons are patents, trademarks, and copyrights.

— The Law of Negotiable Instruments. Negotiable instruments are written promises or requests that certain sums of money be paid to the bearer or to order. Negotiable instruments include promissory notes, checks, and drafts. A businessperson needs to be aware of the obligations each instrument carries as well as of the proper form and various types of endorsements.

— The Law of Bankruptcy. This law governs bankruptcy proceedings. If a business is no longer capable of meeting its financial obligations, it may petition voluntarily or be petitioned for by creditors to be declared bankrupt. There are three forms of bankruptcy. In one form, Chapter 7 bankruptcy, the business is liquidated. In the second form, Chapter 11 bankruptcy, the business is allowed to reorganize, stay in operation, and pay off its creditors over a period of time. The final type of bankruptcy, Chapter 13, offers the business an extended period of time to pay off its debts to creditors.

— The Law of Torts. A tort is a private or civil injury or wrong arising from a breach of a duty created by law. Tort law protects from harm either a person or property as a result of either negligent or intentional acts. Business torts may include fraud, slander, unfair competition, combinations to divert trade, and interference with business relations and contracts.

## Before Viewing

— Review the Overview and Learning Objectives for this lesson.
— Read the following assignment from the text *before* watching the television segment:
  Straub and Attner, *Introduction to Business*, Third Edition, Chapter 20, pages 584–599.
— Define the Key Terms listed in the next section.
— Review the Television Focus Questions and take notes on the questions when viewing the program.

## Key Terms

Terms are referenced to a page of the text.

**agent** (p. 592)                              **common law** (p. 588)
**bankruptcy** *or* **insolvency** (p. 598)      **contract** (p. 590)

**copyright** (p. 596)
**crime** (p. 588)
**negotiable instruments** (p. 597)
**patent** (p. 593)
**principal** (p. 592)
**service mark** (p. 595)

**statutory law** (p. 588)
**tort** (p. 588)
**trademark** (p. 595)
**Uniform Commercial Code (UCC)**
   (p. 589)
**warranty** (p. 592)

## Television Focus Questions

1. What does Scott Bradley of Jenkins and Gilchrist include as areas of the law businesspersons need to be aware of?

2. What types of property are identified by Scott Bradley? Why does a person need to know about the law of property?

3. How does Scott Bradley describe a contract?

4. What does Scott Bradley note about obligations and rights involved in a contract?

5. How does Scott Bradley distinguish between the law of contracts and the law of sales?

6. What does a businessperson need to know about negotiable instruments according to Scott Bradley?

7. When does Scott Bradley state that the law of agency applies to business operations? Why does a businessperson need to know about agency?

8. What is a tort according to Scott Bradley? What is the relationship between a tort and a person's liability? What can be included as a tort? What example is given to illustrate a tort?

9. What areas of the law does John Walsh of Trammel Crow Company deal with?

10. What reason does John Walsh give for a businessperson to be knowledgeable of the law of negotiable instruments?

11. What point does John Walsh make about the importance of contracts?

12. What does John Walsh cite as the consequences of not knowing the law? What example is provided to illustrate the point?

13. What does John Walsh mean by, "It's sometimes not fair, but a businessman who doesn't understand the law can't cry unfairness"?

14. What is the area of the law that is consistently the most difficult according to John Walsh?

15. How does John Walsh try to ensure that he is in compliance with the law?

# After Viewing

- Review and answer the Television Focus Questions. If you are uncertain of the information, or missed a point, view or listen to the program again.
- Review the Key Terms from your text and be sure you understand the Learning Objectives for this lesson.
- Take the Self-Test to check your understanding of the concepts presented in this lesson. Compare your answers to the Answer Key located at the end of the lesson. If you answered incorrectly, the key provides a reference point so you can review the material.
- Extend your learning by completing the Business in Action and Your Business Portfolio sections of the lesson.

# Self-Test

## True/False

**T F 1.** Statutory law is a body of law based on records of early English court decisions settling disputes that involve people and property.

**T F 2.** The Uniform Commercial Code is a comprehensive body of business law that encompasses various kinds of transactions to ensure business transactions will be handled consistently from state to state.

**T F 3.** To be valid a contract must be in writing.

**T F 4.** Under the law of property a warranty can be granted.

**T F 5.** A negotiable instrument is a written promise or request that certain sums of money be paid to the bearer or to order.

**T F 6.** According to John Walsh, vice-president of Trammel Crow Company, the law of negotiable instruments deals with negotiating contracts.

**T F 7.** The law assumes a person understood the contract if he or she signed it.

## Multiple Choice

**1.** Which of the following is an element of a contract?
   **a.** offer
   **b.** acceptance
   **c.** consideration
   **d.** all of the above.

2. The law of sales deals only with
   a. real property.
   b. intangible real property.
   c. tangible real property.
   d. tangible personal property.

3. Which of the following is a classification of property governed by the law of property?
   a. real property
   b. legal property
   c. convertible property
   d. moveable property

4. Of particular importance to businesspeople in the area of property law is
   a. civil rights.
   b. criminal rights.
   c. copyrights.
   d. educational rights.

5. For an instrument to be negotiable, it must be
   a. in writing.
   b. signed by the maker.
   c. for a specific sum of money.
   d. all of the above.

6. According to Attorney Scott Bradley of Jenkins and Gilchrist, the law of agency has to do with
   a. negotiating contracts.
   b. conducting the affairs of one person through another person.
   c. selling tangible property.
   d. creating liability.

7. A form of bankruptcy in which a group of creditors petitions the court to declare a debtor bankrupt so they may collect at least part of their claims is called
   a. creditors' bankruptcy.
   b. bottom-line sellout.
   c. voluntary bankruptcy.
   d. involuntary bankruptcy.

## Business in Action

This exercise is designed to have you investigate the elements of the law that affect business operations.

**Step 1.** Interview the owner or a top-level manager of a small- to medium-sized business in your community that sells lawn mowers, furniture, lamps, or sports equipment. Ask the following questions:

— What elements of business law are involved in your business operations (i.e., contract, sales, agency, property, and negotiable instruments)?

— When and under what circumstances do you or your business become involved in contracts?
    **a.** Who prepares the contract?
    **b.** How is the contract reviewed before it is finalized?

— What items sold by your business require a contract? Why?

— What warranties are given by your business on the items sold?
    **a.** What proof of warranty is given to the customer?
    **b.** Who prepared this warranty?

— What negotiable instruments do you or your business become involved with?
    **a.** What problems, if any, have you encountered?
    **b.** How have you resolved these problems?

— What obligations are incurred by you or your business by employing salespersons to sell your product to the public?

— What does a businessperson need to know about law?

— Do you use a lawyer? If so, how important is the lawyer in your operation?

**Step 2.** Interview the owner or a top-level manager of a small- to medium-sized business in your community that builds homes or office buildings, sells and installs sprinkler systems, or repairs television sets or home appliances. Ask the same questions as in Step 1.

**Step 3.** Record the answers to these questions, summarize your interviews, and discuss the results.

## Your Business Portfolio

This exercise is designed to help you identify personal involvement with the elements of business law.

**Step 1.** Following is a list of the elements of business law. For each element determine your personal involvement by completing the appropriate information.

— Contracts
    **a.** What property or service have you purchased by signing a contract?
    **b.** Why was it necessary to sign a contract for this particular activity?
    **c.** On that contract identify the six required areas of a contract.

— Sales
   **a.** Identify ten items that you have purchased without signing a contract.
   **b.** Why was it unnecessary to sign a contract in these situations?

— Property
   **a.** Identify at least three warranties you have received after purchasing property.
   **b.** Are there any elements of the purchase that are not warranted?
   **c.** How long was the warranty period?

— Negotiable Instruments
   **a.** Identify the negotiable instruments you have used (i.e., notes, checks, drafts).
   **b.** Under what circumstances was each used?
   **c.** What specific requirements accompanied each?

— Agency
   **a.** Identify instances in which you have been involved with an agency arrangement (i.e., realty, travel, stockbroker).
   **b.** What obligations did the agent have to you and to the principal?

**Step 2.** Summarize and discuss your findings.

# Answer Key

The Answer Key provides a reference for each question: T (text page), TG (Telecourse Guide page), or V (video program).

## True/False

1. **F** (T 588)
2. **T** (T 589, 590, TG 180)
3. **F** (T 590)
4. **F** (T 592–597)
5. **T** (T 597, TG 181)
6. **F** (V)
7. **T** (T 592)

## Multiple Choice

1. **d** (T 590, 591)
2. **d** (T 592, TG 180)
3. **a** (T 592, TG 181, V)
4. **c** (T 593, TG 181, V)
5. **d** (T 597, 598)
6. **b** (V)
7. **d** (T 599)

# Lesson

# 24

# The Environment: Business and the Economy

## Learning Objectives

After studying this lesson, you should be able to:

1. Explain the interdependence of businesses in our economic system.
2. Describe the effect of business competition on available factors of production.
3. Explain the concept of the business cycle.
4. Define the concept of inflation and its impact on a business and the business system.
5. Define the concept of recession and its impact on a business and the business system.
6. Relate the function of the Federal Reserve System to the supply of money for the economy and business.
7. Describe the role of the Federal Reserve System in establishing monetary policy and the effect of monetary policy on business.
8. Describe the role of the federal government in establishing fiscal policy and the effect of fiscal policy on business.
9. Explain the interactions of monetary and fiscal policies as they affect the business economic climate (including such factors as interest rates and employment).

## Overview

This is the fourth of a five-part sequence of lessons describing the environment a business must function within. This lesson focuses on the critical elements of the economy that influence the operations and decision making of a business. **187**

A businessperson can develop a unique marketing plan, be a shrewd financier, hire quality employees, and produce a product with maximum efficiency, and still not survive. Why? A business cannot control the economy, but the economy affects business—sometimes with devastating results. What a business does and how it does it are influenced by economic factors. Those factors include the interdependent nature of business in our economy, the business cycle, and the actions of both the Federal Reserve System and the federal government to moderate the economy through monetary and fiscal policy.

A starting point to understanding the impact of the economy on business decision making and operation is to understand that businesses are interdependent. Businesses depend on one another as customers and suppliers. As part of our mixed or modified capitalistic system, businesses (as well as households and government) are customers for other businesses. As a result of these supplier-customer relationships, the actions taken by each independently influence the success or failure of the others. If a business that is the major customer of a small-business supplier goes out of business, there is a very high probability the smaller business will follow suit. If the economy is unfavorable to one segment of business, it will not be the only business segment adversely affected.

When examining business interdependence, it is important to note that businesses are not only customers and suppliers for each other, but that all businesses need the same resources (land, labor, capital, and entrepreneurship). As a result, all businesses compete against one another for the factors of production. This illustrates how business influences labor costs (salaries), cost of materials, and the cost of financing (capital). If one business increases the wages it pays for labor, other businesses in the same field may follow. In addition, to pay the higher wages the business may have to raise the prices of its goods, which in turn forces a customer or company to pay more. The lesson a businessperson should draw from this concept is that businesses are connected in our economy through their customer-supplier relationships and their competition for resources.

Critical to decision making and a business's operation is the *business cycle:* a pattern, or cycle, of events in the economy. When plotted on a graph it is, on the surface, a series of ups and down in the operation of the economy. Closer inspection reveals periods of expansion resulting in growth of business operations, periods of contraction in which business operations slow down, a trough during which the cycle reaches a low point, and a peak phase in which output is at its maximum in the economy. These periods of economic expansion and contraction influence the operations of a business and its decision making in the areas of employment, income, output, and prices. During periods of expansion employees are hired, businesses are growing, and few businesses are failing. During periods of contraction unemployment increases, businesses cut back on their production of goods, and a significant number of businesses go out of business.

**188**     Two terms associated with the business cycle are *inflation* and *recession.*

Inflation usually occurs on the up side of a business cycle as the cycle approaches its peak; it is a general increase in the levels of prices over a period of time. Inflation impacts the prices paid for goods and services. It requires more money to purchase the same amount of goods and services (i.e., the price of goods and services is inflated). This means the factors of production cost more; the cost to a business for the same amount of land, labor, and capital will be greater.

Recession describes a low point of business activity and a low point in the business cycle. It is a slowdown or decline in the activity. Consumers buy less of the products businesses have produced. Businesses in turn reduce output and lay off workers, thus creating unemployment. The workers in turn can buy fewer products, which further slows the economy. To sell the products they have produced, suppliers lower or maintain prices.

For a businessperson the business cycle and its accompanying periods of expansion, contraction, and price inflation are facts of life—they are going to occur. The questions then become: How severe will the decline be? How long will the expansion phase be? When will recovery take place? In an attempt to ease the ups and downs in the business cycle, two tools are available—monetary and fiscal policy controlled by the Federal Reserve System and the federal government respectively.

The Federal Reserve System was created by Congress and made responsible for managing the nation's supply of money and credit. The "Fed," as it is known, is the major influence on the money supply for the economy and, ultimately, business. It directly affects the monetary base, the total amount of currency held by the nonbanking public (businesses and individuals), plus resources held by banks. The monetary base in turn is the foundation of our money supply.

The Fed monitors the economy and the business cycle and through its actions attempts to moderate the fluctuations of the business cycle (including taking action to lessen the rate of inflation). The Fed opens and closes the valve on the money supply for business as well as consumers and government. By applying monetary policy, through its various tools, it makes money and credit easy or difficult to obtain and, eventually, to spend. During periods of contraction the Fed can take actions to make money easy to obtain, thus increasing the supply of money and stimulating the economy. On the other hand, during periods of rapid expansion the Fed may wish to slow the economy down—to limit either the possibility of inflation or the actual rate of inflation. It is able to do this by decreasing the availability of money and credit.

The Federal Reserve System has three primary tools to work with in implementing monetary policy: open market operations, reserve requirements of member banks, and discount rates established for loans to member banks. By utilizing these tools the Fed is able to influence businesses' decisions. If money is easily available, business can acquire money for its operations from banks at a lower cost. This in turn allows and encourages expansion, growth, employment, and the development of new products. When the money supply is tight, business makes "hard" decisions on what it can and will do.

The federal government also attempts to influence the economic climate.

Through the development and implementation of fiscal policy the federal government influences business decision making. Government fiscal policy relates to deliberate changes in taxes and government spending for the purpose of changing capital investment, income, and employment.

In government spending the objective is to put money into the economy to affect business and consumer spending. This deliberate action stimulates the economy, creates jobs, and generates income. Rather than injecting money directly into the system through spending, the government may attempt to stimulate demand for goods and services, the supply of goods and services, or both, by modifying the tax structure. If the government lowers the rate of income tax, less money goes to the government, thus increasing the opportunity for business and consumers to spend more for goods and services, to invest in businesses, or to save. If the government increases the tax rates, the opposite will be true.

A businessperson must be aware of the purposes, tools, and effect of monetary and fiscal policies as they are implemented in the economy. When used in combination they send a clear message to the businesses in our economy. They impact the supply of money, actual spending, and production, which affects employment (more or fewer jobs available) and income. If more money is available through government spending and lower taxes (fiscal policy), more is invested in our economy and businesses. If money is easier to obtain through our banking system, more can be invested in our economy and businesses (monetary policy). If too much money is available, however, and there is too much spending and not enough production, it leads to inflation.

Obviously a business or businesses cannot control the economy. But a business must understand the nature of our economic system—that businesses are interdependent, the health of one may affect many more, and the actions they take for the factors of production affect each other. In addition, the economy operates in a cyclical pattern that must be monitored because it influences business planning. Finally, businesspersons must be aware of the attempts to regulate the business cycle through monetary and fiscal policy and of what those actions *may* result in.

## Before Viewing

- Review the Overview and Learning Objectives for this lesson.
- Read the following assignment from the text *before* watching the television segment:
  Straub and Attner, *Introduction to Business*, Third Edition, Chapter 13, pages 358–373.
- Define the Key Terms listed in the next section.
- Review the Television Focus Questions and take notes on the questions when viewing the program.

## Key Terms

Terms are referenced to a page of the text.

**certificates of deposit (CDs)** (p. 369)

**check** *or* **demand deposit** (p. 364)

**Consumer Price Index (CPI)** (p. 365)

**cost-push inflation** (p. 365)

**demand-pull inflation** (p. 365)

**discount rate** (p. 373)

**Federal Reserve Act of 1913** (p. 369)

**inflation** (p. 365)

**money** (p. 362)

**open market operations** (p. 372)

**prime rate of interest** (p. 368)

**reserve requirement** (p. 372)

**savings account** *or* **time deposit** (p. 365)

## Television Focus Questions

1. What term does Professor Lester Thurow of the Massachusetts Institute of Technology use to describe the periods of high and low activity in business?

2. What specific effects does Professor Thurow state the business cycle has on business? Why may a company still go broke even if it is managed perfectly?

3. How does Professor Thurow define inflation? Recession?

4. What does Professor Thurow say is the effect of inflation and recession on business? What examples does he provide to illustrate this point?

5. What does Walt Humann, president of Hunt Oil Company, note are the effects of the business cycle on Hunt Oil Company's diverse operations?

6. What three potential responses to the business cycle does Walt Humann suggest?

7. How have inflation and recession affected Hunt Oil Company according to Walt Humann?

8. What two mechanisms does Professor Milton Friedman of Stanford University identify that are used to provide stability to the economic environment?

9. According to Professor Friedman, what does monetary policy deal with? What determines the total quantity of money in the country?

10. What are the three instruments of monetary policy noted by Professor Friedman?

11. How does monetary policy affect the business climate according to Professor Friedman?

12. What is the direct effect noted by Professor Friedman of spending in the economy on the business?

13. What does Professor Friedman include as components of fiscal policy?

14. What are the purposes of fiscal policy noted by Professor Friedman?

15. What effect of monetary policy is described by Walt Humann?

**191**

16. What example does Walt Humann use to describe the impact of government fiscal policy?

17. What two strategies for operating successfully in the economic environment are offered by Professor Thurow?

18. What three strategies for business to adopt are suggested by Walt Humann?

**View the television program "The Environment: Business and the Economy."**

# After Viewing

— Review and answer the Television Focus Questions. If you are uncertain of the information, or missed a point, view or listen to the program again.

— Review the Key Terms from your text and be sure you understand the Learning Objectives for this lesson.

— Take the Self-Test to check your understanding of the concepts presented in this lesson. Compare your answers to the Answer Key located at the end of the lesson. If you answered incorrectly, the key provides a reference point so you can review the material.

— Extend your learning by completing the Business in Action and Your Business Portfolio sections of the lesson.

# Self-Test

## True/False

T F 1. What a business does and how it does it are influenced by economic factors.

T F 2. Businesses depend on each other as suppliers and customers.

T F 3. According to Professor Lester Thurow of the Massachusetts Institute of Technology, the *business cycle* is a term applied to the periods of high and low activity in business.

T F 4. Inflation usually occurs on the down side of the business cycle.

T F 5. The "Fed" is the major influence on the money supply for the economy and, ultimately, for business.

T F 6. The discount rate is the amount of discount the federal reserve gives to member banks when it borrows money.

T F 7. When monetary and fiscal policies are used in conjunction with each other, they impact the supply of money, actual spending, and production.

## Multiple Choice

1. Which of the following describes the relationship of businesses in the economic system?
   a. Businesses are independent of each other.
   b. Large businesses dominate small businesses.
   c. Businesses are interdependent.
   d. Businesses cooperate with each other.

2. When making decisions and operating the business, a businessperson
   a. must control the economic variables.
   b. must be aware of the economy and its impact.
   c. can minimize the economic variables.
   d. should always adjust the forecast of economists.

3. Which of the following describes the business cycle?
   a. It has minimal consequences for a businessperson.
   b. It influences decision making in the areas of employment and expansion.
   c. It is a theoretical concept with minimal application to business.
   d. It influences banking but has minimal impact on industry.

4. According to Professor Lester Thurow of the Massachusetts Institute of Technology, the business cycle
   a. affects business investment decisions.
   b. increases spending.
   c. reduces taxes.
   d. forces bargaining concessions.

5. A situation requiring more money to purchase the same amount of goods can be described as
   a. a recession.
   b. a contraction of the business cycle.
   c. fiscal policy.
   d. inflation.

6. Monetary policy
   a. is designed to control imported goods.
   b. is administered by the Federal Reserve System.
   c. is a factor that increases the rate of inflation.
   d. forces the government to reduce its tax structure.

7. According to Walt Humann, president of Hunt Oil Company, monetary policy can be felt
   a. by a reduction in retirement income.
   b. through a lack of cooperation by businesses.
   c. through an increased cost of capital.
   d. by an increase in competition in the marketplace.

**193**

## Business in Action

This exercise is designed to have you investigate the impact of the economy on business.

**Step 1.** Interview the owner or top-level manager of a medium-sized retail business in your community and ask the following questions:

- Over the last 6 months what economic factors have influenced your business decisions and operations?
- What specific decisions in terms of growth or expansion, employment, wages, and inventory have you made as a result of these economic factors?
- Are you aware of any attempts by the Federal Reserve System to increase or decrease the money supply through monetary policy?
- Are you aware of any attempts by the federal government to stimulate or slow down the economy?
- How do you monitor the economy to keep up with the changing environment?
- What process do you use to incorporate information about the economy in your decision making?

**Step 2.** Interview the owner or top-level manager of a medium-sized manufacturing business in your community and ask the questions identified in Step 1.

**Step 3.** Record your answers to the interviews and discuss your findings.

## Your Business Portfolio

This exercise is designed to involve you in the impact of economic variables on the business environment.

**Step 1.** For a 2-month period monitor *The Wall Street Journal, Business Week,* or the business section of your local newspaper for information regarding the economy and the impact of the economy on business.

**Step 2.** Maintain a log citing the topic of the article, the article's highlights, and the areas of business affected. An example would be:

| Topic | Information | Impact |
|---|---|---|
| Reserve requirements | Federal Reserve System raised reserve requirements for member banks from 10% to 13%. | Member banks will have less to lend. Business will have a difficult time acquiring money. |

**Step 3.** After monitoring the economic environment, prepare a summary. It should include:

— The stage of the business cycle the economy is in (expansion, peak, contraction, trough).
— The effect of the position of the business cycle on business in general.
— The effect of the position of the business cycle on specific industries.
— The actions taken by the federal government to regulate the business cycle.
— The actions taken by the Federal Reserve to regulate the business cycle.

## Answer Key

The Answer Key provides a reference for each question: T (text page), TG (Telecourse Guide page), or V (video program).

### True/False

1. **T** (TG 188, V)
2. **T** (TG 188)
3. **T** (V)
4. **F** (TG 189, V)
5. **T** (TG 189)
6. **F** (T 373, V)
7. **T** (TG 190)

### Multiple Choice

1. **c** (TG 188)
2. **b** (TG 190, V)
3. **b** (TG 188, V)
4. **a** (V)
5. **d** (T 365, TG 189, V)
6. **b** (TG 189, V)
7. **c** (V)

# The Environment: Business and Social Responsibility

## Learning Objectives

After studying this lesson, you should be able to:
1. Define social responsibility.
2. Explain the evolution of social responsibility.
3. Explain the rationale for organizations to accept social responsibility.
4. Describe the socially responsible actions taken by business in the following areas: small-business investment, education and training, employment opportunities for minorities and women, the handicapped in business, urban renewal, community involvement, environmental concerns, energy concerns, employee health, consumer protection, and ethical conduct of business.
5. Explain the importance of the evaluation of social policy.

## Overview

This is the fifth in a series of lessons describing the environment that influences the decision making and, ultimately, the operations of a business. Once again, a business does not operate in a vacuum. It is a functioning member of a community, of a state, and of a nation at large. The expectations, values, and needs of society should be evaluated by a business as it functions. Business decisions should be made with full knowledge of their impact on society. The overriding goal of profit must be pursued within a social framework. What then is social responsibility?

Social responsibility is a belief that, as organizations and managers function, their decisions should be made within the confines of both social and economic considerations. This belief comes from a recognition that business organizations exert considerable influence on the general well-being of society. Their actions, products, and services directly affect the environment, the welfare of their suppliers, and their customers' standard of living. In pursuing its ultimate goal of profit, business must turn its attention to matters of the public need that it can pursue simultaneously. Social responsibility is not a philanthropic activity; it is investing in society in the long-range. A business makes an investment for its long-range profitability and for society's.

Why should a business accept the idea of social responsibility and integrate it into its organizational philosophy and actions? Quite simply, a strong, viable society contributes to the general health and well-being of an organization. It is inconceivable to think of business being strong while society in general is ailing. Companies with a high social consciousness further their own goals when they help strengthen the social structure. In turn, it builds a hospitable environment for tomorrow's business success. Social objectives actually enhance a firm's profitability over the long run. In addition, business has the talent and resources to partner with society and government to address the pressing problems affecting everyone's future.

The concept of social responsibility did not happen overnight. It has evolved over the years through three observable stages. These stages, representing degrees of acceptance of the concept of social responsibility and involvement by companies, are the enlightened self-interest phase, the social awareness phase, and the social responsiveness phase. Each phase presents a movement toward more active partnering with society.

In meeting its social responsibility objective business has taken, and will continue to take, actions to address the needs of society. These specific areas, though addressed by business, still provide opportunities for business action: small business involvement, education and training, employment opportunities for minorities and women, the handicapped in business, urban renewal, community involvement, environmental concerns, energy concerns, employee health, consumer protection, and ethical conduct of business.

Not all businesses have addressed all these areas; nor should they. A business needs to evaluate its resources—financial, human, and technical—and direct its energies to those that are most pressing as well as to those the company is best equipped to focus on. What a business cannot and should not do is abstain from addressing the needs of society. To do so will eventually result in an inhospitable and unhealthy environment.

If the organization is committed to socially responsible actions and social responsibility, both an implementation plan and a means to evaluate results are needed. Implementing social responsibility requires that social responsibility be established as the job of all managers—in essence, fixing the area of social responsibility in the organization and developing policies for implementing programs. In turn, these actions of managers and the programs need to be evaluated.

## Before Viewing

— Review the Overview and Learning Objectives for this lesson.

— Read the following assignment from the text *before* watching the television segment:
Straub and Attner, *Introduction to Business*, Third Edition,
Chapter 21, pages 612–638.

— Define the Key Terms listed in the next section.

— Review the Television Focus Questions and take notes on the questions when viewing the program.

## Key Terms

Terms are referenced to a page in the text.

**code of ethics** (p. 632)

**ethics** (p. 630)

**minority enterprise small-business investment companies (MESBICs)** (p. 618)

**recycling** (p. 625)

**social audit** (p. 629)

**social responsibility** (p. 616)

**urban revitalization programs** (p. 621)

**van pooling** (p. 627)

## Television Focus Questions

1. How does Professor John Matthews of Harvard University respond to the question, "Is there a danger of overreacting to some abuses of social responsibility and indicting the business community as a whole?"

2. How has the view of social responsibility evolved over the years according to Professor Kenneth Goodpaster of Harvard University?

3. Why does Professor Goodpaster state that it would be a good thing for business to have an external focus? How is this focus changing?

4. How does Professor John Matthews describe the social responsibility of business?

5. What four reasons are cited by Professor Matthews for a business to be concerned about social responsibility?

6. What does Dr. James Worthy, a director of Control Data, state is the meaning of social responsibility at Control Data?

7. Why has Control Data become involved in social responsibility programs according to Dr. Worthy? What specific programs has it undertaken?

8. What does Dr. Worthy think the results of these programs will be on society?

9. What does Professor John Matthews state is necessary to make these social responsibility programs work?
10. What does Dr. James Worthy cite as the commitment of Control Data?
11. What does Professor Kenneth Goodpaster point out as a monitoring device a company may use for its programs on social responsibility?
12. What specific monitoring device is noted by Professor Matthews?
13. How does Control Data monitor its programs according to Dr. Worthy?

**View the television program "The Environment: Business and Social Responsibility."**

# After Viewing

— Review and answer the Television Focus Questions. If you are uncertain of the information, or missed a point, view or listen to the program again.
— Review the Key Terms from your text and be sure you understand the Learning Objectives for this lesson.
— Take the Self-Test to check your understanding of the concepts presented in this lesson. Compare your answers to the Answer Key located at the end of the lesson. If you answered incorrectly, the key provides a reference point so you can review the material.
— Extend your learning by completing the Business in Action and Your Business Portfolio sections of the lesson.

# Self-Test

## True/False

T   F   1. Social objectives actually enhance a firm's profitability over the long term.

T   F   2. The concept of social responsibility has evolved over a number of years.

T   F   3. Business' commitment to social responsibility in employment opportunities for minorities and women is to meet the letter of the law.

T   F   4. Many large businesses are committed to hiring handicapped workers but are not prepared to modify the physical work environment.

**199**

T  F  5. Recycling is an attempt by business to meet its social responsibility commitment in the area of environmental maintenance.

T  F  6. According to Dr. James Worthy of the Control Data Board of Directors, social responsibility is viewed as paternalism and philanthropic activities.

T  F  7. The social audit is a report on the social performance of a business.

## Multiple Choice

1. Which of the following describes the operating environment of business?
   a. independent
   b. interdependent
   c. insecure
   d. challenging

2. Which of the following describes social responsibility?
   a. It is best evidenced by supporting local charities.
   b. It requires major budget allocations.
   c. It is a belief that business decisions should be made within the confines of both economic and social considerations.
   d. It places demands on an organization.

3. Included in the rationale supporting social responsibility is the thought that
   a. it is required by society.
   b. government regulations mandate it.
   c. what is good for society is good for the business firm.
   d. social responsibility is everybody's job.

4. Which of the following is a phase in the evolution of social responsibility?
   a. the legalistic phase
   b. the enlightened self-interest phase
   c. the governmental phase
   d. the social dilemma phase

5. Which of the following is an area businesses have focused on in social responsibility?
   a. small-business investment
   b. education and training
   c. the handicapped in business
   d. all of the above

6. According to Dr. James Worthy of the Control Data Board of Directors, the impact of social responsibility on society includes
   a. productive employment for people.
   b. rewarding careers for people.

   c. basic educational skills for people.
   d. all of the above.
7. As an area of social responsibility urban revitalization programs
   a. are directed at building new cities.
   b. require donations by all companies.
   c. provide new jobs and improve the city's economic health.
   d. redirect resources from the business.

# Business in Action

This exercise is designed to have you investigate the status of business' social responsibility in your community.

**Step 1.** Identify a small, medium, and large business in your community.

**Step 2.** Interview the owner or top-level manager in each and ask the following questions:

   — What is your company's philosophy toward social responsibility?
   — How has your company put this philosophy into action?
   — What resources has the company allocated to meet these commitments?
   — What expectations does the company have for its managers and operating employees for individual participation in social responsibility activities?
   — How are these expectations communicated to management and employees?
   — What support is given to the employees for their individual participation?

**Step 3.** Record the answers to these questions.

**Step 4.** Analyze the degree of commitment and types of involvement according to the size of the firm.

**Step 5.** Summarize and discuss your findings.

# Your Business Portfolio

This exercise is designed to involve you as a representative of your organization in fulfilling its commitment to social responsibility in your community.

**Step 1.** Review the potential areas for social responsibility discussed in this lesson's reading assignment.

**Step 2.** Identify three areas from this list that (1) are compatible with the philosophy of the company you work for and (2) are recognized needs in the community.

**Step 3.** Identify and contact appropriate social agencies, community groups, or governmental organizations that can serve as resources to identify specific participation needed by companies and individuals.

**Step 4.** Identify specific actions and resources your company could provide to address these needs.

**Step 5.** Construct a plan to ensure that these actions become a commitment by the organization and that the results are evaluated.

## Answer Key

The Answer Key provides a reference for each question: T (text page), TG (Telecourse Guide page), or V (video program).

### True/False

1. **T** (T 616, TG 197)
2. **T** (T 616, TG 197)
3. **F** (T 620)
4. **F** (T 621)
5. **T** (T 625)
6. **F** (V)
7. **T** (T 629)

### Multiple Choice

1. **b** (T 614)
2. **c** (T 616, TG 196, 197)
3. **c** (T 616)
4. **b** (T 616, 617, TG 197)
5. **d** (T 618–622, TG 197)
6. **d** (V)
7. **c** (T 622)

# Lesson

# The Challenge of High Technology

## Learning Objectives

After studying this lesson, you should be able to:

1. Explain the nature of high technology.
2. Explain the impact of high technology on business and the work force.
3. Describe the impact of high technology on work and the workplace, the worker, and the manager.
4. Explain the impact of high technology on society.

## Overview

This lesson is the first of a three-lesson series exploring the challenges facing a business and the business community. High technology, productivity, and business on an international scale pose challenges to managers and provide opportunities for innovation, creativity, and problem solving. Each challenge must be addressed, rather than avoided. Each may cause changes in the way a business operates, in its entire organizational structure, in its managerial value system, and in its allocation and utilization of resources. The starting point and the focus of this lesson is to explore the challenge of high technology: its nature, its impact on business and the work force, and its impact on work, the work setting, workers, managers, and society at large.

Just what is high technology? Is it surrounded with mystery, suggesting test tubes in the laboratory and scientists working in guarded surroundings? Actually, *high technology* is a term that is used to describe a combination of ingredients: science, creativity, research, resources. High technology is both an outcome of devices and systems (robotics, telecommunications, information systems) and an environment.

High technology is not something that has just happened in the last 10 or 20 years. It has been with us in the form of the steam engine, the semiconductor, the computer in all variations, the cordless telephone. All these high-technology devices have required a combination of science, research, creativity, and resources. These devices or inventions described as high technology all have something in common besides these four ingredients. They all have provided leverage to their users; they have provided power by their ability to accomplish their tasks far faster or with far greater efficiency than the devices they replaced.

High technology has been with us and will continue to be with us. Since that is the case, it is not what is being described as high technology at the moment that is important—that will change. Rather, what is important is the impact high technology is having, and will have, on business, the business setting, workers, managers, and society at large. This impact presents a challenge.

The major impact of high technology on business in general and the work force can be described in one word—change. High technology has brought change into every area of business.

— There is more access to information. This requires a change in the way the information is processed as well as a need for more rapid decision making.

— Traditional job structures and career paths are no longer applicable. Traditional jobs may no longer be needed. This in turn changes job families and the normal means of job progression.

— Equipment and systems become outdated quickly. This has forced business to change purchasing practices, or to move to leasing arrangements, to remain current with the state-of-the-art devices.

— As high technology changes, the job skills needed in these jobs changes. No longer are car mechanics working with the ignition systems of old: it is now a solid state system, which in turn requires that the technician use more conceptual skills.

— The composition of the work force is changing and will continue to change. As more and more high-technology automation moves into the work setting, the ratio of blue-collar to white-collar jobs will change, more staff experts will be needed, and the number of line managers will decrease (fewer people to manage but more technical advice will be needed).

These are some of the changes in business in general and in the work force at large. Now let's examine the impact of high technology in the work setting. How will work and the workplace, the worker, and management be affected?

The impact of high technology will differ depending on the type of business and industry that experiences it. Generally, high technology should remove the mundane, repetitive nature of many jobs and allow the worker to be utilized for the more creative aspects of work. Much of the preparation for work, the collection of information, and its sorting and computation can be done through technology. In other areas the actual repetitive tasks will be done by technology (robots welding on the assembly line). In turn, workers will work with the artificial intelligence of the equipment, design applications for information, and perform work high-technology equipment cannot do.

The workplace as we know it will be affected by high technology. Traditional equipment has been and will continue to be replaced. (Typewriters, in many cases, have been replaced by word processors.) This in turn will change the construction of offices and factories, introduce new sounds and eliminate old ones, change where work will be done (at home rather than the traditional office setting, for instance), and allow people in different geographic locations to work on a project with one another (in computer interaction as well as telecommunications).

What is and will be the impact of high technology on the workers? The answer to that can be found in the manner workers respond to the change. Workers will be subject to change—change in the way work is done, the skills required, and the knowledge necessary to do the work, in addition to any changes in the physical work setting. These series of changes can and will create stress and fear. If the worker fights the new technology, it will be traumatic, but if the change is accepted and worked with, the stress should be minimized. A number of effects are certain: the worker will be required to constantly update education and training or become obsolete; the worker will face the demands of learning new skills; and the worker will be required to accept the changes as they continue to accelerate.

The impact of high technology on managers and managerial practices will be as extensive as on the worker the manager will be asked to supervise. First, management styles will change as the environment becomes more automated. In addition, the traditional management role in some settings may change— managers will be more involved in work than in managing. Also, the skill requirements—human, technical, and conceptual—will remain, but managers at lower levels will be required to use more conceptual skills than in the past. Another impact may be to flatten out the organization structure: the number of levels of middle management we now have will be reduced. Finally, the biggest impact of all—managers at all levels in the organization will need extensive training in the technologies that will affect their work environment. If this is done they will be able to embrace the technology and not fear it.

Society at large will be impacted by high technology. The structure of society as we know it—upper, middle, and lower—may be modified. The quality of life will be affected for many people. Education as we know it will undergo major changes. People in general will need to be able to adapt and to focus on opportunities. High technology is indeed a challenge.

**205**

## Before Viewing

- Review the Overview and Learning Objectives for this lesson.
- Read the following assignment *before* watching the television segment: *Telecourse Study Guide to The Business File,* Overview, pages 203–205.
- Review the Television Focus Questions and take notes on the questions when viewing the program.

Please note: There are no Key Terms for this lesson.

## Television Focus Questions

1. What two factors does Dr. Richard Byrne of the Byrne Group include in describing high technology?
2. What does Dr. Byrne cite as the impact of high technology on the business climate? What is the difference between a change and a breakthrough?
3. What does Dr. Byrne point out that influences the impact of high technology on people?
4. What does Dr. Byrne note is the critical message from the high-technology environment for people to focus on?
5. What does Dr. Byrne propose as two potential impacts of high technology on the workplace?
6. What specific example does Larry Dalke, maintenance foreman at Chaparral Steel, give in emphasizing the impact of high technology on the work environment?
7. What two specific examples of the impact of high technology on the workplace are provided by Jerry Redmon, director of engineering for telecommunications at Rockwell International?
8. What does Dr. Richard Byrne state could be the potential impact of high technology on the worker? What determines the positive or negative results?
9. What does Jerry Redmon cite is the impact of high technology on Rockwell's engineers? What impact does high technology have on an individual's knowledge?
10. What does Larry Dalke state is the impact of high technology on the worker?
11. What does Dr. Byrne describe as the impact on managers?
12. What does Jerry Redmon see as the impact on his managers?
13. What does Larry Dalke indicate is the impact of the availability of information through high technology on his managers? What example does he provide?

14. What does Professor Arthur Harkins of the University of Minnesota state is going to be the impact of high technology on society at large?

15. How will high technology impact the quality of life according to Professor Harkins?

16. What does Professor Harkins cite as changes to be made in education as a result of the high-technology environment?

17. What does Professor Harkins point out as keys to successfully negotiating these changes?

**View the television program "The Challenge of High Technology."**

## After Viewing

— Review and answer the Television Focus Questions. If you are uncertain of the information, or missed a point, view or listen to the program again.

— Be sure you understand the Learning Objectives for this lesson.

— Take the Self-Test to check your understanding of the concepts presented in this lesson. Compare your answers to the Answer Key located at the end of the lesson. If you answered incorrectly, the key provides a reference point so you can review the material.

— Extend your learning by completing the Business in Action and Your Business Portfolio sections of the lesson.

## Self-Test

### True/False

T  F  1. *High technology* is a term that applies only to inventions and systems.

T  F  2. High technology is a phenomenon that applies only to the 1980s and 1990s.

T  F  3. In the high technology environment the traditional job structures and career paths are no longer applicable.

T  F  4. Much of the preparation for work, the collecting of information, and its sorting and computation can be done through technology.

T  F  5. According to Jerry Redmon, director of engineering for Rockwell International, high technology limits the number of people involved in a project.

T   F   **6.** One of the results of the rapid change associated with high technology is that it can create fear and stress in the worker.

T   F   **7.** Managers in a high-technology environment will *not* need to change their leadership styles.

## Multiple Choice

**1.** Which of the following is an ingredient or element of high technology?
  **a.** language
  **b.** secrecy
  **c.** research
  **d.** all of the above

**2.** The devices or inventions that are described as high technology all have the following in common:
  **a.** high cost
  **b.** flexibility
  **c.** the ability to leverage
  **d.** automation

**3.** According to Dr. Richard Byrne of the Byrne Group, high technology's impact on business in general has
  **a.** modified decision making.
  **b.** created a bureaucracy.
  **c.** been primary in introducing change.
  **d.** created new levels of management.

**4.** Which of the following describes the impact of high technology on the nature of work?
  **a.** Work will become simplified for all workers.
  **b.** The more mundane, repetitive elements of work will be done by technology.
  **c.** Work will become more complicated.
  **d.** All work will be done by robots.

**5.** According to Jerry Redmon, director of engineering for Rockwell International, the work done by engineers
  **a.** is becoming more simplified.
  **b.** is being made more difficult by competition.
  **c.** will be more creative and less routine.
  **d.** will focus on results not methods.

**6.** High technology will have an impact on the workplace by
  **a.** changing where the work is performed.
  **b.** removing the need for factories and offices.
  **c.** automating all procedures.
  **d.** increasing the level of activity.

**7.** In the high-technology environment
   **a.** there will be a need for more managers.
   **b.** the three skills of managers—human, technical, and conceptual—will be expanded to include communications skills.
   **c.** the number of middle managers will decrease.
   **d.** the need for managers will be reduced by artificial intelligence systems.

# Business in Action

This exercise is designed to have you investigate the impact of high technology in the work setting.

**Step 1.** With the aid of your college or public library, research the impact of high technology on the work setting. Focus on the following areas:

— The Impact of High Technology on the Composition of Work and How It Is Performed
   **a.** What work and elements of work will be the responsibility of people?
   **b.** What work and elements of work will be the responsibility of technological devices?
   **c.** What objectives will be involved in assigning work to technology?

— The Impact of High Technology on the Work Setting
   **a.** What specific changes will be made in the design of work settings?
   **b.** What modifications will be seen in the actual workplace?
   **c.** What environmental changes will take place in the work setting regarding noise, socialization, and space allocation?

— The Impact of High Technology on the Worker
   **a.** What skills will the worker in a high-technology environment need?
   **b.** How often will the worker need to update learning to stay current?
   **c.** What psychological factors may influence a worker in a high-technology environment?
   **d.** What special requirements will there be for the worker whose work setting becomes his or her home?

— The Impact of High Technology on Managers and Management Practices
   **a.** What specific demands will be placed on managers in a high-technology environment?
   **b.** What will be necessary to enable a manager to make the transition to a high-technology setting?
   **c.** What balance of technical, human, and conceptual skills will be necessary for managers?

**Step 2.** Record the answers and discuss your findings.

## Your Business Portfolio

This exercise is designed to involve you in the challenge of high technology.

**Step 1.** Review the concept of high technology developed in this lesson (devices and systems that provide leverage).

**Step 2.** Identify in your home and workplace ten examples of high technology and indicate what impact they have made in that setting. An example would be:

*High Technology Device*

1. Microwave oven

*Impact*

1. a. Reduced time to prepare food
   b. Saved energy
   c. Provided leisure time
   d. Required learning new concepts

**Step 3.** Discuss the impact of high technology from your experiences.

## Answer Key

The Answer Key provides a reference for each question: T (text page), TG (Telecourse Guide page), or V (video program).

True/False

1. F (TG 203)
2. F (TG 204, V)
3. T (TG 204)
4. T (TG 205)
5. F (V)
6. T (TG 205)
7. F (TG 205, V)

Multiple Choice

1. c (TG 204)
2. c (TG 204, V)
3. c (V)
4. b (TG 205)
5. c (V)
6. a (TG 205, V)
7. c (TG 205)

# Lesson
# 27

# The Challenge of Productivity

## Learning Objectives

After studying this lesson, you should be able to:

1. Define the concept of productivity and explain how productivity is determined.
2. Describe the evolution of productivity.
3. Compare American productivity efforts with those of other countries.
4. Identify and explain the factors that affect productivity.
5. Describe the changes necessary to improve productivity.
6. Describe the methods to improve productivity.

## Overview

A major challenge facing a business as well as the total business community is in improving productivity. Productivity is the basic measure of the efficiency of a business—in essence, it is increasing the output for each dollar invested in the business. In other words, productivity refers to how much output we get for a given amount of input.

Productivity usually is expressed as a ratio between output and input. It is the result of dividing input into output. Output is measured in dollars or units, while input is measured in hours. An example of measuring productivity is provided by a worker who works 8 hours (input) and produces 40 widgets (output). This worker's productivity index is 5 (40 divided by 8). On a national scale, the U.S. Department of Labor's Bureau of Labor has developed a ratio to measure the nation's productivity. It is a ratio of our national output of goods and services (the dollar measure of the market value of the nation's output in goods and services) divided by the total hours of human labor needed to produce the product.

211

Productivity is important to a manager, a company, an industry, and a nation's economy. All are concerned with the efficient use of resources. All are concerned that there is increasing output for each dollar invested in the business. This concern is justified. Why?

If you turn the clock back to the Industrial Revolution, the United States began to emerge as a leading nation in production capacity and in productivity. By employing sound management techniques, constantly improving its technological base, and channeling the energy and talents of its work force, the United States moved to the forefront in productivity. Historically, it has been one of the most productive countries in the world.

Beginning in the 1960s, the picture began to change. The U.S. rate of growth in productivity decreased. (It increased at a decreasing rate.) While productivity increased an average of 4.2 percent annually in 1960 through 1966, it increased *only* an average of 2.1 percent annually in 1973 through 1979. Many European countries and Japan surpassed this country's productivity rate.

Why did this happen? To answer this question, we must look at it from both an overall environmental, or macro, view and an organizational, or micro, view. From a macro viewpoint a number of factors have influenced the productivity picture including government actions, labor actions, and the economy.

— Government Actions. Government actions, from the legislatures to the regulatory agencies, affect all elements of business operations. Through the process of having to comply, and reporting on this compliance, businesses must complete volumes of reports. The burden of this paperwork adds to the cost of doing business and lessens productivity. Every dollar and every hour spent on government paperwork is one less for production of goods and services.

— Labor Actions. Labor action has two facets: individual employees and organized labor. Individual employees have been accused of lessening productivity by not approaching the job with the same degree of enthusiasm as previously—of wanting or expecting more but not wanting to produce more for it. Organized labor also has been accused of affecting productivity through higher wage demands and demands for fewer hours of work for the same output. In addition, the traditional adversarial role has been singled out as a source of delay or blockage.

— Economic Factors. Economic conditions have ultimately influenced productivity. These factors are intermingled and create a domino effect on productivity. The high rate of inflation (goods and services have an inflated value) has been fueled in part by the government's huge deficits, which create the need to borrow billions each year to finance present and past deficits. These dollars, taken from capital markets, are in turn unavailable to consumers and businesses who need them to finance their purchases and investments. Thus, less money is available for capital improvements. Heavy borrowing by the federal government to pay the deficits also drives up interest rates. Higher interest rates create demands for higher wages.

Companies that give raises then have to raise prices. The same goods are produced and sold for higher costs but not with an increase in productivity. In addition, higher interest rates cause businesses to delay spending. Less money invested in businesses means less capital equipment is purchased, which can result in obsolete equipment and less productivity.

These are all general contributing factors to the productivity problem, but not the entire story. The real cause is found by examining the organization itself and management specifically.

Management has tended to sacrifice long-term planning for short-term gains, has had frequent executive turnover that results in changes in company direction and plans, and has had a tendency to diversify operations that in turn leads to spending executive time trying to learn new, unfamiliar operations.

In addition to these global approaches of management, the problem can be traced to management attitudes and practices—not managing the human resources of the organization as effectively as possible. Management has not created a climate that fosters participation, open communication, or utilization of the expertise and creativity of individual workers. On the contrary, management has failed to work with the productivity ingredients that it can influence. Government actions, labor organizations, and inflation are not within the control of operating managers, but their approaches in utilizing human resources are. Operating management has contributed to the productivity problem by:

— Providing rewards to employees that are not the result of additional output or productivity.
— Creating an inefficient communication system that results in delays, frustrations, and improper information for decision making.
— Applying the same management tools and styles that were effective years ago, but may not be based on the motivational needs of today's workers.
— Refining jobs to a degree of specialization that results in less satisfaction and more boredom.
— Utilizing practices that have been made obsolete by accelerating technology.

What can be done to attack the productivity dilemma? Knowing that management cannot control the government, labor, or the economy, it needs to focus on the controllable variable—the organizational climate. Changes need to be made by management to improve productivity. Specifically top-level management must:

— Develop a climate of trust within the organization to remove the idea of us versus them.
— Provide for open communication and keep a continuous flow of communication and information going in the organization.
— Commit to productivity as a value of the organization.

— Actually get involved in productivity efforts.
— Convince lower-level managers that productivity is a priority of the organization.
— Ensure that long-range strategic plans are made in conjunction with and in support of productivity efforts.
— Ensure that productivity is part of the company's business plan and budget.
— Ensure that rewards are the result of performance.

Once top-level management has committed to these changes and has begun to create an organizational climate, lower levels of management must build on the momentum. Managers need to focus on managing their subordinates and managing the work of the subordinates. Specifically the methods management must use include:

— Matching a subordinate's skills and abilities to the job he or she is performing. This will result in a more efficient use of resources *and*, more importantly, provide for a more motivated and less frustrated employee.
— Focusing performance appraisals on accomplishments or results rather than personality or how well an employee can get along with the boss.
— Reinforcing the importance of results in a job by utilizing reward systems based on performance, not entitlements.
— Implementing a participative management system in which the talents of individuals are brought into the decision-making process and decisions are made at the lowest possible levels in the organization.
— Fostering a leadership that focuses on team performance and group participation.
— Ensuring that communication is upward, downward, and vertical in the organization and that it deals with reality.
— Developing decisions into precise plans of action that give the organization a logical blueprint for achieving its objectives.
— Utilizing a management by objectives program to establish clear objectives that are understood by all members of the organization.
— Incorporating quality circles as a participative management tool where applicable.
— Practicing time management and both human and industrial engineering techniques.

In summary, the key to productivity—to efficiency and effectiveness in the organization—is to practice sound planning, organizing, staffing, directing, and controlling.

214

# Before Viewing

- Review the Overview and Learning Objectives for this lesson.
- Read the following assignment *before* watching the television segment:
  *Telecourse Study Guide to The Business File,*
  Overview, pages 211–214.
- Review the Television Focus Questions and take notes on the questions when viewing the program.

Please note: There are no Key Terms for this lesson.

# Television Focus Questions

1. How does Robert Waterman of McKinsey and Company define productivity?
2. What does Professor William Ouchi of UCLA note is the significance of the loss of productivity? What will happen to the United States if this trend is not altered?
3. What does Robert Waterman state is the main problem in the decline in the growth of productivity?
4. What factors are cited by Professor William Ouchi that reinforce Robert Waterman's belief?
5. What two major changes does Robert Waterman claim must be made to make organizations more productive?
6. What change needs to be made according to Professor William Ouchi? What is the first step toward this change?
7. What does Professor Ouchi state is necessary to build an atmosphere of trust? How does a leader become transparent?
8. Where does Robert Waterman say the push for productivity must start?
9. What does Robert Waterman cite is necessary for the idea of productivity to become important to the entire organization? How does "management by wandering around" contribute to productivity?
10. According to Professor William Ouchi, how does a company ensure that the first-line manager accepts productivity as a priority?
11. What specific action does Professor Ouchi note that an operating manager can take to make an increase in productivity happen?
12. What specific actions can be taken by management according to Robert Waterman?
13. What point does Robert Waterman make about taking suggestions seriously?

14. According to Professor William Ouchi, what two elements are common ingredients for companies that have improved their productivity?

15. Is productivity a long- or short-range proposition according to Professor Ouchi?

**View the television program "The Challenge of Productivity."**

## After Viewing

— Review and answer the Television Focus Questions. If you are uncertain of the information, or missed a point, view or listen to the program again.

— Be sure you understand the Learning Objectives for this lesson.

— Take the Self-Test to check your understanding of the concepts presented in this lesson. Compare your answers to the Answer Key located at the end of the lesson. If you answered incorrectly, the key provides a reference point so you can review the material.

— Extend your learning by completing the Business in Action and Your Business Portfolio sections of the lesson.

## Self-Test

### True/False

T F **1.** Productivity is the basic measure of the efficiency of a business.

T F **2.** Productivity is important to a manager, a company, an industry, and a nation's economy.

T F **3.** The rate of productivity growth in the United States has consistently increased.

T F **4.** According to Professor William Ouchi of UCLA, the productivity situation has significant implications for the standard of living.

T F **5.** Labor has improved productivity by continually agreeing to wage increases based on increased output and productivity.

T F **6.** Management has negatively affected productivity by sacrificing long-range planning for short-term gains.

T F **7.** Top-level management is responsible for ensuring that long-range strategic plans are made in conjunction with and in support of productivity efforts.

## Multiple Choice

1. Which of the following is a measure of productivity?
   a. dividing total salary of employees by units produced
   b. the ratio of wages earned to wages paid
   c. the ratio of one's total output to the total education of the work force
   d. dividing the output in terms of units or dollars by the input in terms of hours

2. Productivity in the United States has shown
   a. a decrease.
   b. a decrease in the rate of growth.
   c. an increase compared with other nations.
   d. a restructuring of measurements.

3. Which of the following has influenced the productivity problem?
   a. government actions
   b. economic factors
   c. labor actions
   d. all of the above

4. According to Robert Waterman of McKinsey and Company, the prime cause of the productivity problem is
   a. delay in investment in equipment.
   b. labor's arbitrary positions in regard to productivity.
   c. the influence of Japanese imports.
   d. management's attitude.

5. Which of the following describes the role of economic factors in the productivity problem?
   a. The economy is uncertain, which leads to poor decision making on productivity.
   b. High interest rates result in the tendency to make money less available for business to invest in capital equipment.
   c. Inflation has minimal impact on productivity.
   d. Increasing wages result in more investment in productivity measures.

6. According to Robert Waterman of McKinsey and Company, productivity
   a. is the responsibility of every worker.
   b. is the responsibility of management only.
   c. must start at the top of a company.
   d. cannot be measured.

7. Which of the following is a method recommended to improve productivity?
   a. overseeing all activities employees perform
   b. matching a subordinate's skills and abilities to the job he or she is performing
   c. requiring all work to be documented
   d. eliminating all unnecessary technology

**217**

## Business in Action

This exercise is designed to have you investigate the productivity dilemma and potential solutions for the dilemma.

**Step 1.** Identify two large businesses in your community and interview a top-level manager in each using the following questions:

— What is the rate of productivity of your organization over the last four years (increased, remained the same, decreased)?
— What do you believe are the external (government, economy, labor) and internal (management) factors that have resulted in this position?
— Does your organization have a long-range plan directed toward monitoring and improving productivity? Why?
— What has top management done *purposefully* to improve the productivity of the organization?
— What have lower levels of management done voluntarily to improve productivity?
— What have lower-level managers been instructed to do to improve productivity?

**Step 2.** Summarize your answers and discuss the results of the interviews. In your discussion be sure to address:

— Management's awareness of the productivity problem.
— Specific factors noted that influence productivity.
— Whether any *planned* productivity actions are in use.

## Your Business Portfolio

This exercise is designed to involve you in the challenge of productivity.

**Step 1.** Identify a company where you previously worked or are now employed to evaluate for productivity performance.

**Step 2.** Using the following factors, determine if they are present in the work environment. If they are, explain why you think so. If they are not, explain why you believe they are not. Explain the effect of each factor on productivity.

| Factor | Present | Absent |
|---|---|---|
| A climate of trust is present. | _____ | _____ |
| Open communications exist. | _____ | _____ |
| Productivity is a value of the organization. | _____ | _____ |

| Factor | Present | Absent |
|---|---|---|
| Top management is actively involved in productivity efforts. | _____ | _____ |
| Plans are made to support productivity efforts. | _____ | _____ |
| Subordinates' skills and abilities are matched to job demands. | _____ | _____ |
| Performance appraisal is based on results, not personalities. | _____ | _____ |
| Rewards are based on results. | _____ | _____ |
| Participation in decision making is practiced. | _____ | _____ |
| Communication is upward, downward, and vertical. | _____ | _____ |
| Communication deals with reality. | _____ | _____ |
| Decisions are translated to usable plans of action. | _____ | _____ |
| Management by objectives is used to establish clear objectives. | _____ | _____ |
| Time management is a value of the organization. | _____ | _____ |

**Step 3.** Provide a summary of your analysis and determine the readiness of your organization to meet the challenge of productivity.

# Answer Key

The Answer Key provides a reference for each question: T (text page), TG (Telecourse Guide page), or V (video program).

True/False

1. **T** (TG 211)
2. **T** (TG 212)
3. **F** (TG 212, V)
4. **T** (V)
5. **F** (TG 212)
6. **T** (TG 213)
7. **T** (TG 214)

Multiple Choice

1. **d** (TG 211, V)
2. **b** (TG 212, V)
3. **d** (TG 212)
4. **d** (V)
5. **b** (TG 212, 213)
6. **c** (V)
7. **b** (TG 214)

# Lesson

# The Challenge of Business on an International Scale

## Learning Objectives

After studying this lesson, you should be able to:

1. Describe the scope and importance of international trade.
2. Explain the major concepts involved in international trade: balance of trade, balance of payments, exchange rate, and absolute and comparative advantage.
3. Explain why a business chooses to participate in international business.
4. Explain the levels of involvement in international business a firm may select.
5. Identify and explain the barriers to international trade.
6. Identify and describe the conflicts that occur between an international business and the host and home countries.

## Overview

This lesson, The Challenge of Business on an International Scale, is the third of three lessons focusing on the challenges facing business. For those businesses that choose to enter the international business arena, special challenges await. There are the unique challenges of language, culture, and politics as well as the critical decision on what alternative to use—export office, joint venture, licensing. It is a brand new set of rules with its own intricacies.

"Going international" is not something out of the ordinary for a business. The scope of international trade is enormous. With the advent of efficient transportation and communication systems the world has become a giant international department store. For many countries international trade *is* their business.

That's business on an international scale, but why would a company take the giant step into the international business arena? The most obvious answer and the prime motivator is profit. Companies constantly evaluate the allocation of their resources to produce profits. One alternative in the decision-making process that is becoming more enticing is international target markets for profitable operation.

When companies engage in international business they discover it has a language all its own. These major concepts include balance of trade, balance of payments, and exchange rate, as well as the concepts of absolute and comparative advantage. These concepts describe elements of international business and in some instances affect the actual operations of companies as well as nations.

Making the decision to embark in international business necessitates a second decision—how? A business may select from a number of alternatives. Each in turn increases the level of the commitment of the organization's resources. The alternatives include export department or foreign intermediary, foreign licensing, joint venture, foreign-operated sales branches, and wholly owned subsidiaries. The ultimate involvement is to become a multinational corporation—one that operates on an international level, is based in one country but has operations in other countries, and does a substantial amount of its total business in other countries.

Companies that become involved in international business are confronted with barriers that can hamper their operations. These barriers include language, customs and cultural differences, currency conversion, and protectionist practices. Protectionist practices are the result of a philosophy of trade focused on protecting domestic industries from foreign competition. The main tools of protectionism include tariffs, embargoes, and quotas.

In addition to these barriers, an organization engaged in international business may encounter conflicts with both the home country (where they are originated and headquartered) and the host country (where they have affiliated). Both these conflicts arise out of questions of economics and power. They result in concerns of allocation of resources, where operations should be conducted, who owns the facilities, and ultimately, who makes decisions about the company.

# Before Viewing

— Review the Overview and Learning Objectives for this lesson.
— Read the following assignment from the text *before* watching the television segment:
  Straub and Attner, *Introduction to Business,* Third Edition,
  Chapter 19, pages 554–581.
— Define the Key Terms listed in the next section.
— Review the Television Focus Questions and take notes on the questions when viewing the program.

## Key Terms

Terms are referenced to a page of the text.

**absolute advantage** (p. 563)
**balance of payments** (p. 559)
**balance of trade** (p. 558)
**comparative advantage** (p. 563)
**devaluation** (p. 561)
**diversification for stability argument** (p. 573)
**dumping** (p. 569)
**economic alliances** (p. 576)
**embargo** (p. 575)
**exchange rate** (p. 561)
**Export-Import Bank** (p. 576)
**exporting** (p. 558)
**foreign-operated sales branch** (p. 567)
**foreign trade intermediary** (p. 566)
**General Agreement on Tariffs and Trade (GATT)** (p. 576)

**home industries protection argument** (p. 573)
**importing** (p. 558)
**infant industries protection argument** (p. 573)
**International Monetary Fund** (p. 576)
**licensing** (p. 566)
**multinational corporation** (p. 567)
**national security argument** (p. 574)
**production sharing** (p. 569)
**protectionism** (p. 573)
**quota** (p. 575)
**revaluation** (p. 561)
**tariff** *or* **import duty** (p. 575)
**wage protection argument** (p. 574)
**wholly owned foreign subsidiary** (p. 567)

## Television Focus Questions

1. According to Professor Fariborz Ghadar of George Washington University, what percent of the world's gross national product is directly related to international business and trade? In the United States, what percent of jobs is directly related to international trade and investment?

2. What main reason is given by Professor Fariborz Ghadar for an individual company to become involved in the international arena? What five specific motivations do companies have for becoming involved in international business?

3. What reason is given by John Jorden, administrative vice-president of international operations for Core Laboratories, for Core Laboratories becoming involved in international trade? How important are international operations in generating revenue?

4. What options or levels of involvement has Core Laboratories used in international business according to John Jorden?

5. What reason is given by John Jorden for Core Laboratories becoming involved in joint ventures?

6. What does Professor Fariborz Ghadar include as potential cultural barriers? What examples are given to illustrate cultural barriers?

7. What examples are provided by John Jorden of cultural taboos to avoid in international business?

8. What does Michael Jordan, president of Frito-Lay, Inc., state is a reason why companies violate cultural barriers in international business?
9. What suggestion is made by Michael Jordan to avoid this mistake? What two examples are provided to illustrate the point?
10. What reason is given by Professor Fariborz Ghadar for conflicts between multinational companies and the host country?
11. What three categories of conflict between the multinational company and the host country are noted by Professor Fariborz Ghadar?

**View the television program "The Challenge of Business on an International Scale."**

# After Viewing

— Review and answer the Television Focus Questions. If you are uncertain of the information, or missed a point, view or listen to the program again.
— Review the Key Terms from your text and be sure you understand the Learning Objectives for this lesson.
— Take the Self-Test to check your understanding of the concepts presented in this lesson. Compare your answers to the Answer Key located at the end of the lesson. If you answered incorrectly, the key provides a reference point so you can review the material.
— Extend your learning by completing the Business in Action and Your Business Portfolio sections of the lesson.

# Self-Test

## True/False

T   F   **1.** Multinational business is primarily an element of the future.

T   F   **2.** The exchange rate can be established by government action or through market conditions.

T   F   **3.** "Going international" can be motivated by the potential to take advantage of an established demand for American goods.

T   F   **4.** According to John Jorden, administrative vice-president of international operations for Core Laboratories, the international section of Core's operations provides an insignificant amount of revenue for the corporation.

T   F   **5.** If a firm uses interpreters, language is eliminated as a barrier to international trade.

T   F   **6.** The home industries protection argument is the argument that trade with other nations will cause domestic industries to lose their customers to foreign competitors, forcing firms out of business and throwing workers out of jobs.

T   F   **7.** Conflicts between multinationals and host countries center on the fact that multinationals have different goals than do the governments of the societies in which they begin operations.

## Multiple Choice

**1.** Which of the following describes international trade?
   **a.** It has become an increasingly important part of world activity.
   **b.** It increases the variety of goods available.
   **c.** It encourages interaction and understanding.
   **d.** All of the above.

**2.** If exports exceed imports the
   **a.** exchange rate decreases.
   **b.** exchange rate increases.
   **c.** balance of payments is favorable.
   **d.** balance of payments is unfavorable.

**3.** When a company has a monopoly on a product or can produce it at the lowest cost, it is known as
   **a.** unfair competition.
   **b.** a controlled market.
   **c.** a black market.
   **d.** an absolute advantage.

**4.** Which of the following is a reason for a company to become involved in international trade, according to Professor Fariborz Ghadar of George Washington University?
   **a.** to stabilize trade
   **b.** to exploit comparative advantage
   **c.** to test-market new products
   **d.** to minimize losses

**5.** An alternative for involvement in international business that shares ownership of the foreign operations with foreign nationals is a
   **a.** foreign intermediary.
   **b.** joint venture.
   **c.** licensing arrangement.
   **d.** foreign-operated sales branch.

**6.** A multinational corporation
   **a.** may work in partnership with host country firms.
   **b.** may form joint ventures with host country firms or governments.
   **c.** may establish operations on its own.
   **d.** may do all of the above.

7. A trade barrier that restricts the quantity of a foreign product that can be brought into a country for resale is
   a. a tariff.
   b. a quota.
   c. an absolute advantage.
   d. a comparative advantage.

# Business in Action

This exercise is designed to have you investigate the barriers to international trade.

**Step 1.** For a 2-month period, monitor the political or protectionist barriers to international trade by reading the newspaper, *Business Week,* and *Nation's Business.* (The latter two publications should be available in your school or public library.) During your research period monitor and record the following:

— Statements made by members of Congress, economists, and businesspeople in favor of or opposed to protectionism.
— Statements made by representatives of nations in response to these comments.
— Actions taken by the United States in placing, increasing, removing, or modifying quotas, embargoes, or tariffs.
— Proposed effect of the quotas, tariffs, or embargoes.
— Actions taken by the producers of the products that have quotas, tariffs, or embargoes placed on their goods.

**Step 2.** Summarize and analyze your findings.

**Step 3.** Identify the industries most directly affected by these actions and explain why these industries either need or do not need protection in your opinion.

# Your Business Portfolio

This exercise is designed to identify the impact of international business in your life.

**Step 1.** Develop a list of thirty items you have purchased for your personal, family, or home use. For example: radio, television, dress shoes, athletic shoes, linens, dresses, suits.

**Step 2.** Identify the country or countries in which each one, or its components, was manufactured. Follow this example chart for recording your answers.

| Product | Country |
|---------|---------|
| chocolate | Holland |
| television | Japan, United States |

**Step 3.** Summarize your findings.

## Answer Key

The Answer Key provides a reference for each question: T (text page), TG (Telecourse Guide page), or V (video program).

| True/False | | Multiple Choice | |
|---|---|---|---|
| 1. | **F** (T 556) | 1. | **d** (T 558) |
| 2. | **T** (T 561) | 2. | **c** (T 558, 559) |
| 3. | **T** (T 565) | 3. | **d** (T 563) |
| 4. | **F** (V) | 4. | **b** (V) |
| 5. | **F** (T 571) | 5. | **b** (T 566) |
| 6. | **T** (T 573) | 6. | **d** (T 567) |
| 7. | **T** (T 578) | 7. | **b** (T 575, V) |